SMALL-SCALE SHEEP KEEPING

Jeremy Hunt is an agricultural writer and journalist specializing in livestock production and pedigree breeding. A lifetime's interest in all aspects of stock keeping and good husbandry has concentrated more recently on running a small flock of pedigree sheep. He draws on his extensive practical experience gained from many years of keeping a host of different breeds of stock to produce this guide for the first-time sheep keeper. Jeremy Hunt lives with his wife and two sons in the Ribble Valley in Lancashire and writes each week in *Farmers Weekly*. He is a regular columnist and feature writer for *Country Life* magazine and contributes to other country and livestock publications.

D0921129

also available from Faber

GOAT HUSBANDRY (fifth edition) by David Mackenzie
SMALL-SCALE POULTRY KEEPING by Ray Feltwell
RACING PIGEONS

Small-scale Sheep Keeping

Jeremy Hunt

faber and faber
LONDON · BOSTON

First published in 1997
by Faber and Faber Limited
3 Queen Square London WC1N 3AU

Typeset by Faber and Faber Ltd
Printed in England by Mackays of Chatham plc, Chatham, Kent

The illustrations on pp. 6, 33, 48, 67, 69 and 70 are based on drawings
in *Sheep Management and Production* by Derek Goodwin (1971)

Jeremy Hunt is hereby identified as author of this
work in accordance with Section 77 of the Copyright,
Designs and Patents Act 1988

A CIP record for this book
is available from the British Library

ISBN 0–571–17893–6

2 4 6 8 10 9 7 5 3 1

Contents

ONE

Making a Start

Pedigree and Commercial Options – Where to Seek Advice –
Buying from Auctions and Private Flocks – Important Conformation
Points – Buying Proven Breeding Stock – What to Look for in Sheep
Dentition – Lambs for the Butcher or the Breeder

Selecting a breed is not always the first consideration for the new, small-scale sheep keeper. It is more than likely that the breed has selected him or her! How many times have we heard stories of those who have become totally captivated by a particular breed? It is often the sheep that prompts the move to the house with a few acres and not the house that prompts the purchase of the sheep. So, for some newcomers to sheep keeping, this chapter may serve as a reference to the main British breeds including those classified as 'rare' as well as the most popular commercial crosses and Half-breds. For those already smitten by a particular breed, this chapter may inspire a 'second string'; for those yet to start their own flock it will hopefully act as a guide and enable them to compile a short list of those breeds most suited to individual circumstances and experience.

Once a sheep addict always a sheep addict, and for those of us who admire a whole host of breeds it can be very difficult not to end up with a 'collection' of sheep. This is not to be recommended; it can lead to disappointment and disaster borne of self-inflicted complicated management as the shepherd strives to meet the specific needs of a mixed flock.

My advice would be to select one breed and commit yourself wholeheartedly to it. Running two breeds on a small scale does add a measure of problems, particularly at tupping, but for those who have split loyalties or who simply thrive on variety, go for it, but be prepared to rein back quickly if you feel you are over-committed.

For those about to embark on keeping pedigree sheep as a new venture and with no fixed ideas about breeds, it is advisable to visit at least one of the major agricultural shows and see a comprehensive parade of the very best of British sheep. If you are so far down the road to becoming a sheep keeper that you follow this piece of advice, your visit to the show must be tempered with caution. Remember that sheep on show are, for the most part, the result of week after week of careful preparation and feeding and many hours of skilful trimming. The sheep you see in the ring are in their best bib and tucker; show sheep are often a far cry from the way these breeds look at home in their working clothes. When a breed does take your fancy, go and talk to one of the exhibitors at the show. You will find sheep breeders very tolerant of newcomers and if they feel your circumstances – in terms of acreage, time available and experience – are not suited to their particular breed they will tell you so; then it is back to the drawing-board. Hopefully, by the time you have read this chapter and weighed up the pros and cons of all the breeds, you will have a broad grasp of those most likely to suit your situation.

Do not go for glamour to start with. Some breeds could charm the cheque-books out of buyers' pockets but remember that the most eye-catching sheep are probably, though not always, those which demand the most attention. Spend time visiting flocks; breeders are usually only too pleased to show off their stock at home; and remember that 'home' is where you will see sheep in their natural surroundings and where you can most effectively evaluate their suitability for your own few acres.

Before deciding on a breed, it is appropriate to look at where to buy your sheep. Autumn is the main auction season for both pedigree and commercial sheep sales, although by mid-July some pedigree breeds are already well under way with their main events. The autumn season gives buyers the chance to buy females after lambs have been weaned but also to buy gimmer (female) lambs born that year. Rams will also be on offer, but more of that later. It has also become popular in recent years to stage sales of pedigree in-lamb ewes during the winter months. Breeds like the Suffolk, Texel, Charollais and Hampshire Down now hold such sales. These are a good way for newcomers to buy in sheep already mated and certified 'in-lamb', but I would strongly recommend any newcomer taking this route to establishing a flock from scratch to seek the advice of an experienced shepherd. Unless you feel totally confident, it is always useful to invite someone experienced to any sale from which you intend to buy sheep.

All sales bearing the word 'official' in their title are run by the relevant breed society, which means that all sheep on offer will be vetted and inspected on arrival at the sale. Any found to have serious conformation faults – particularly important when buying rams – are rejected and not allowed to be sold.

Most of these events will be advertised in the farming press, in such journals as *Farmers Weekly* and *Farmers Guardian*, but each breed society will be able to inform you of the dates and venues. A full list of all breed societies can be obtained from the National Sheep Association. Buyers do have a degree of protection afforded by the auction system and there is no doubt that competitive bidding is guaranteed to make the adrenalin flow.

Sad to say, in the heat of the moment and at the mercy of very adept auctioneers, the thrill of a bidding battle can all too often turn the most cautious purchaser into a reckless buyer. Securing new stock at auction is great fun but it can cost dear. Buying privately from a reputable breeder is probably the most sensible way to start and it can often save you the trouble of buying a ram in your first year. Most breeders selling females privately in the autumn will agree to mate them within their own flock; when you take delivery several weeks later you will already be well on the way to your own first crop of lambs. The advantage here, apart from the initial saving in the cost of buying a ram, is that the ewes will be mated to a ram that the breeder feels is best suited to their bloodlines.

By the time you come to buy a ram, which may well be the following year, you will have had almost a year's experience and should feel more confident about taking the important step of buying your first flock sire. Remember that a ram may only be one sheep but he is in effect half the flock.

If you have opted to run a small flock of commercial sheep – say,

North of England Mules, Welsh Mules or some of the continental crosses – there are plenty of sheep for sale at any time of the year. The North of England Mule – a cross between the Blue-faced Leicester and the Swaledale – is the most popular commercial breeding ewe in the UK. Hundreds of thousands of North of England Mules are sold each autumn at special sales but local markets and special sheep fairs will also provide a wide source of stock covering a range of commercial types suitable for the newcomer to sheep keeping.

Commercial ewes will cost you a lot less then pedigree animals, are easily managed and usually trouble free at lambing because over generations they have proved to be a profitable enterprise when run in large numbers. Recent years have seen some new crosses emerge on the farming scene as enterprising flockmasters have tried to come up with a new 'ideal' commercial ewe. Most have failed to meet the needs of modern flock management because commercial ewes not only have to be able to produce a good lamb for the butcher but also have to lamb easily, produce strong lambs, milk well, have good feet and a vigorous constitution. Many of the new crosses have failed in one or more of these qualities and the old favourites like the North of England Mules, the Welsh Mule, the Scotch Half-bred, the Suffolk-cross and the Welsh Half-bred still retain a major slice of the commercial ewe market in the UK. We shall look at the breeding make-up of these Mules and Half-breds in the chapter on sheep breeds.

There will of course be those new sheep keepers who want to start off with a ready-made family and there is plenty of opportunity to buy commercial ewes with lambs at foot in the spring from special sales at auction marts or direct from farmers who advertise their stock for sale. Many people have no aspirations to breed pedigree stock and are satisfied if they produce a good crop of commercial lambs for the butcher. Not all pedigree sheep end up as prize-winners and inevitably some of the also-rans will end up on the hook.

But those who opt for a pedigree flock add an extra dimension to their livestock interest; the level of stockmanship is much higher and the flock will cost more to establish, but the chance of breeding a champion, and possibly selling it for a good price, is the driving force behind pedigree breeding.

What to Look for When Buying Your Sheep

Every breed of sheep has its own individual characteristics. The breed points of the Southdown are a world apart from those of the Swaledale but they are both breeds of sheep and that means there are certain basic standards of conformation that apply. No matter where or how you buy your sheep you should always ensure that the animals you are looking at fulfil the essential conformation criteria that have nothing to do with breed points. Teeth, for instance, are a very important part of any sheep. You may be offered what appear to be wonderful sheep but if they are 'wrong in the mouth' you should avoid them. Not only will this shortcoming affect their own long-term ability to thrive, but they are likely to pass the fault on to their offspring. While this is not critical in commercial sheep bred for the butcher, it is a very important consideration if you are producing pedigree stock. There is nothing more frustrating than breeding a really good sheep only to find that its mouth is faulty. So, what should we look for in a sheep's mouth? You will hear a lot of talk about the 'pad'. This is the gum which forms the upper part of the sheep's mouth and it is essential that the incisor teeth of the lower jaw meet the pad 'level'. A sheep whose teeth jut outwards from the pad is classed as 'overshot' and where the teeth are slanted 'inwards' is termed 'undershot'.

With experience, you will learn to feel for faults in a sheep's mouth simply by taking hold of the animal's chin and gently inserting a thumb to feel for the way the teeth are lying. Once proficient at this method of assessment, you can use it as one of the most unobtrusive ways of checking a sheep's mouth; something that can be useful when wanting to make a discreet check of pedigree stock over which you have a doubt.

The term 'broken mouth' is widely used in sheep circles and denotes animals whose teeth have started to deteriorate, most

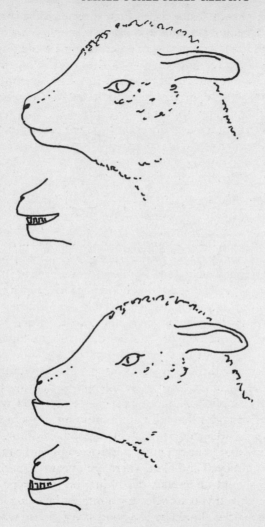

Figure 1. Undershot jaw (top), overshot jaw (bottom)

probably having already lost some of their incisors. Most sheep will retain their incisor teeth until they are at least five years old, so checking dentition is a good way of determining a sheep's age.

Good conformation refers to the way a sheep is put together and there are certain basic faults to watch for. A sheep should stand four-square on straight legs and should move freely, both fore and aft, without any appearance of 'pinning'. This term refers to a turning-in of the legs during movement and although it occurs most commonly in hind movement it can often be a fault in the front action; too many show judges of sheep fail to study front movement as closely as they should and poor front movement is just as serious as incorrect movement behind. The pastern, the lower part of the leg, should be straight and not bent or apparently weak. The leg and pastern should be at right angles to the ground, ensuring that the animal is sound and able to carry its body weight correctly. Weak pasterns, on either front or rear legs, should be closely watched for. A sheep should have healthy feet, free from any signs of disease, and good bone too, which signifies that the animal is well reared and healthy and unlikely to show a weakness in its limbs. Shoulders should be strong and wide and not sharp and bony or A-shaped. If you are buying pedigree sheep, watch out for 'slackness' behind the shoulder; this manifests itself as a dip which occurs just behind the shoulder blade and distorts the appearance of the sheep and destroys the all important level topline. A good sheep has length and well sprung ribs which suggest that 'all within' in terms of room for heart and lungs is adequate to sustain a good constitution. Always make sure that your potential purchases appear healthy and vigorous, bright-eyed and alert. There are of course specific checks that you should undertake, depending on what type of sheep you are buying. If you are selecting a ram for breeding it is obvious that his testicles should be of a good size and firm when handled; you would be quite in order to ask the owner if you can inspect the ram's penis and sheath to ensure there are no problems in this all-important part of his anatomy. Take particular care to check a ram's mouth and remember that while you do not want an aggressive ram, particularly if he may come into contact with children, a ram that shows some spirit is only displaying the very thing you want – dominant maleness. A good-looking ram may look great in the pen at the sale but if he is a lazy worker he will cause you to have a delayed lambing-time. The ram with an outward show of dominance and presence will put that side of his nature to work with your ewes and will ensure that no one misses out on his attentions.

If you are buying mature ewes that have already suckled lambs pay close attention to udders. Any hint of lumpiness or other problem should be avoided. Whether you are buying privately or at a sale always check if the animals have received any routine vaccinations, when they were last treated for worms and when they were most recently dipped. No matter how long you are involved in sheep keeping, you will never forget your first ewes. You may well end up making a few mistakes but invaluable lessons will be learned on the road to becoming a proficient shepherd.

TWO

Choosing a Breed

The First British Sheep – Robert Bakewell's Influence – Terminology Explained – Mountain and Hill Breeds – Shortwool Down Breeds – Shortwool Breeds – Longwool Breeds – Rare Breeds – Half-breds, Mules and Hybrids

The start of sheep keeping in Britain may be traced back 2,000 years to the time of the Romans. They introduced medium-woolled sheep carrying white fleeces, possibly with some Merino influence, but undoubtedly carrying breeding from native Asiatic breeds. When the Romans arrived in Britain in 55BC, the only native sheep were similar in type to the small Soay which had evolved in Scandinavia. The white-woolled sheep and the Soays interbred and eventually produced a type capable of yielding high-quality fleeces. This led to the first exports of British wool which became highly prized for making robes and garments for emperors in Rome.

In the 1,000 years that followed, British sheep breeds evolved into distinctive types and the great abbey estates of the Middle Ages were particularly influential during this period, many probably keeping sheep not unlike the Ryeland breed of today. By the eighteenth century, a more informed outlook was required to meet the growing need for food and it was Derbyshire farmer Robert Bakewell whose dedication and experience formed the bedrock of today's pedigree and commercial sheep industry.

Although concerned with pedigree breeding of all farm livestock, it was from a starting-point with Leicester Longwool sheep that Bakewell made his most significant contribution to British agriculture. His improvement programme, initially producing the Dishley Leicester and later the New Leicester, achieved improved growth rates through careful selection. Many breeds benefited from this pioneering breeder, whose work led to the creation of the Border Leicester and the Blue-faced Leicester, two major components in the development of post-war UK sheep production. Other breeds, like the Devon Longwool, Dartmoor and Wensleydale, also owe much of their present-day appearance to infusions of Dishley Leicester blood.

While Bakewell was busy in the north, another enthusiast had a vision of improvement for short-woolled breeds. John Ellman, from Glynde, near Lewes, Sussex, tackled the short-woolled heath breeds of the South Downs and emerged with a new breed, the Southdown. Widely acclaimed for its mutton, the Southdown was for many years a major influence in the production of sheep meat in the UK.

Today there are over sixty sheep breeds in the UK, including rare breeds and Half-breds. Many people ask why there needs to be so many, but regional sheep breeds have become established in all parts of the British Isles, each one evolving to thrive most efficiently in specific environments of climate and grazing.

Terminal sire breeds are those whose progeny are destined primarily for the butcher. The Suffolk, despite strong challenges from continental breeds, is still responsible for siring over 50 per cent of the prime lamb crop. Suffolk-sired lambs have a reputation for exceptionally high growth rates. The Texel from Holland and the Charollais from France have a keen following as terminal sires. Mules and Half-breds make up the bulk of lowland commercial sheep flocks, although there are still some pure-bred 'non-pedigree' ewe flocks run commercially, particularly in breeds like the Lleyn where inherent high lambing percentage and mothering ability does not need to be improved upon through the hybrid vigour of cross-breeding.

Hill flocks, in the main, are kept pure although there are still many Herdwick and Swaledale flocks in the Lake District where cross-breeding does take place. Scottish Blackface dominate in Scotland, Swaledales in the north of England and Welsh Mountain sheep in Wales. Just to confuse matters for the newcomer, many hill flocks do undertake some cross-breeding with a portion of the flock because the upland farms of the UK are the source of 'Mule' sheep, produced by using Blue-faced Leicester rams on hill ewes. The resultant female 'Mules' are then sold on to lowland farms to be crossed again with a terminal sire to produce a prime lamb for the butcher.

Recent years have seen several breeds arrive in the UK from Europe and there is no doubt that they have had a significant impact. So influential have they become that a separate section will be devoted to the 'continentals' in a later chapter.

The Native Breeds

Mountain or hill breeds

The grazing of millions of sheep on the hill and upland pastures of the UK over hundreds of years has had a major influence on the way this part of our landscape looks today. If your few acres are halfway up a mountain it is likely that your greatest success with sheep will come from keeping those breeds indigenous to that environment. But that is not to say that if you have lowland grazing in kinder climes that a hill breed will not thrive there. The indomitable Herdwick seems just as much at home on Skiddaw as it does in Kent – such is the versatility of our sheep breeds.

Swaledale
A truly hardy breed run in huge numbers in the north of England. The Swaledale is used to produce the North of England Mule by crossing with the Blue-faced Leicester.

Scottish Blackface
The epitome of Highland hill farming. This rugged breed is also used to produce the Scottish Mule by crossing with the Blue-faced Leicester.

Herdwick
A real 'one-off'. Its Nordic ancestry oozes from its knowing eyes, white face and coarse grey fleece. This famous Lake District breed can live to a very old age. One of the hardiest of sheep breeds. Crosses well with terminal sire breeds to produce good prime lambs.

Rough Fell
Another striking breed hailing from the southern edge of the Lake

District. Its coarse wool is favoured for carpet making.

Cheviot
Occurs as both North Country and South Country Cheviots, the former being larger. Both are hardy breeds and despite their classification in the hill section have better than average conformation and can produce extremely good prime lambs.

Welsh Mountain
Numerically the second largest of our hill breeds although the smallest in stature. Lives well on the thinnest of grazings and (along with the Beulah Speckled-faced) is crossed with the Blue-faced Leicester to produce the Welsh Mule.

Derbyshire Gritstone
Another larger type of hornless hill breed that thrives on the wet uplands of the Pennines. Has good conformation and a high-quality wool.

Shortwool Down breeds

This group contains the main breeds used as terminal sires. Selection over many years has produced high growth rate, and breeds such as the Suffolk and Hampshire Down are now involved in the performance-testing schemes to identify superior sires in an effort to improve potential even further.

Suffolk
The predominant terminal sire breed. Pedigree rams can achieve huge prices – 68,000 gns was paid for a ram lamb in 1995. Passes on high growth rate to its cross-bred progeny.

Hampshire Down
A breed increasing in popularity again. Woolly faced and very adaptable to varying grazing conditions. Hampshire Down lambs grow very quickly to twelve weeks and are ideal for early spring lamb production.

Oxford Down
A really big breed that has unfortunately fallen from favour as

demand for large lamb carcasses has declined. Nevertheless, a sheep with great character that deserves more support.

Dorset Down
A breed renowned for its ability to breed out-of-season and produce high-quality prime lamb. Many Dorset-cross ewes are used commercially for this purpose.

Shortwools

Similar in many ways to the Shortwool Down sheep, this group has a number of truly individual breeds that have evolved to meet the requirements of flockmasters in a variety of regions.

Ryeland
A charming breed from Herefordshire with a history going back six centuries. Recently imported bloodlines from Australia have improved the breed, which produces top-quality lightweight prime lambs.

Wiltshire Horn
A 'one-off' breed which carries little or no wool. Despite that, it is a hardy breed.

Kerry Hill
A striking breed with its black-and-white face markings. A challenging breed to produce for the show ring but one that is most adaptable to hill and lowland management.

Clun
A fascinating breed from Shropshire and the Welsh Borders with its unusual 'starey' expression. Once widely used as the dam-breed to produce the English Half-bred by crossing with the Border Leicester.

Lleyn
A wonderful breed from the Lleyn Peninsula in North Wales, it is now becoming very popular even though it was once on the rare-breed list. Prolific, renowned for its trouble-free lambing and easy to manage, this breed looks like becoming a major

force in the British sheep industry.

Longwools

Hornless and with their roots in the most productive arable areas of England, the Longwools are large sheep carrying heavy fleeces. Lambs tend to be later maturing but these are some of the most attractive of all native sheep breeds.

Wensleydale
A large and impressive Yorkshire breed with a blue head. When in full wool they are one of the most attractive of all sheep, carrying a fleece weight of up to 4.5 kg and with an exceptionally long staple. Black Wensleydale sheep now have a strong following.

Teeswater
Similar in type to the Wensleydale and hailing from neighbouring Co. Durham. Now classified as a rare breed, though still used as the sire of the Masham by crossing with Dalesbred ewes.

Blue-faced Leicester
A phenomenon among sheep breeds. Used on over forty different pure-breds as a crossing sire to produce all varieties of Mule, though the North of England, Welsh and Scotch are the most popular. Its unusual appearance, Roman nose and crimped fleece have earned it an almost cult following.

Border Leicester
One of the most famous of British breeds with its large, erect ears, Roman nose and alert demeanour. The sire of the English, Scotch and Welsh Half-bred commercial ewe.

Romney Marsh
A breed with a long history on the marshlands of Kent. A big sheep, still popular in New Zealand, with a reputation for having a tough constitution.

Lincoln Longwool
The largest of British breeds and widely exported throughout the world. Its economic importance to UK sheep farming is now

much reduced, but those who remain loyal to the breed extol its virtues for producing quality prime lambs. A ram fleece weight of 20 kg has been recorded.

Leicester Longwool
Often confused with the Lincoln Longwool, but this breed has 'clean' legs devoid of wool. Its curly and lustrous fleece can weigh up to 6 kg. A major influence on the British Longwool breeds through Bakewell's work.

Rare breeds

The Rare Breeds Survival Trust has achieved much in saving so many of our endangered breeds of sheep. The rare breeds provide the small-scale sheep keeper with a wonderful opportunity not only to establish a flock of pedigree sheep at reasonable cost, but also to become involved in the long-term future of an invaluable sector of British livestock breeding. Newcomers to rare breeds often find it hard to understand why these breeds are so readily available and at such affordable prices if they are so rare. The answer is simply that the RBST has been so successful; but that is not to say that rare breeds are no longer 'rare'. Numbers of many breeds are still very low compared with other mainstream breeds. Although the Hebridean now has its own breed society because its numbers have increased above the 'danger' threshold, there are still only about 1,500 Hebridean breeding ewes owned by around 100 UK breeders. To put that into context, one large hill farm in the Lake District or Scotland might run 3,000 commercial breeding ewes; so rare breeds may achieve a degree of independence but that is not to say they are no longer at risk.

The image many people have of rare breeds is that of the primitive types such as Boreray, Manx Loghtan or Soay, so it often comes as a surprise to learn that breeds like the Leicester Longwool, the Cotswold and the Wensleydale also have rare-breed status.

Hebridean
A black breed of great versatility. Easily managed and thrives on a wide variety of grazings.

Soay

The smallest of the primitives. Very active with attractive brown, chocolate or tan fleece colour. A tough little character hailing from the island of St Kilda.

Castlemilk Moorit

Its tan fleece and deer-like expression adds to the charm of this primitive sheep. A lot tougher than its delicate form suggests.

Manx Loghtan

The word Loghtan (pronounced lock-tan) means mouse-brown and describes the fleece colour of this popular primitive which can be either two- or four-horned.

Shetland

No longer considered rare, this is one of the success stories of the RBST. This breed's soft fleece and varied colours make it very popular among smallholders and hand-spinners.

The Jacob

It is difficult to categorize this breed, but its popularity among small-scale sheep keepers earns it individual attention. The Jacob has a fascinating history and is believed to hail from the Middle East. Once a rare breed in the UK, it now has a huge following and in recent years has improved greatly in terms of conformation and overall quality. The Jacob, which can occur as two-horned, multi-horned and even polled (no horns), is not only one of the most attractive of British sheep breeds with its black-and-white fleece, but the ewes are prolific and milky, make great mothers and as a breed are extremely hardy. Although the breed has an active society and exhibiting Jacobs is very popular, this is far more than just a 'pretty sheep'. Jacobs are a commercial proposition for the small-scale flockmaster who wants to keep attractive sheep in the paddock but still produce a good-quality prime lamb.

Mules, Half-breds and hybrids

Commercial sheep production in the UK is based on producing

Figure 2. Suffolk ram. Photo by Douglas Low

Figure 3. Hebridean ewe.

Figure 4. The Jacob ram. Photo by Douglas Low

Figure 5. A show-winning Texel ewe. Photo by Douglas Low

prime lamb. The two main components of that system are:

(1) a terminal sire that will breed lambs that grow well and have good conformation to meet the demands of the butcher for lean meat and plenty of it; and
(2) a ewe that is easily managed, lambs easily, milks well to rear twins comfortably, is attentive to her offspring, has a reputation for being healthy and vigorous and will not 'wear out' too soon.

Terminal sires are pure breds – Suffolk, Charollais, Texel or similar. But the commercial ewe market is now dominated by crossbreds known as Mules and Half-breds.

By far the most popular, as mentioned earlier, is the North of England Mule which combines the hybrid vigour of the Blue-faced Leicester as its sire and the Swaledale as its dam. The resultant female Mule (male Mule sheep are castrated and sold as prime lamb) is well proven as a top-class commercial ewe. The advantage of such crossing to produce a female with good commercial potential has also given rise to Scotch and Welsh Mules, both of which are proving increasingly popular.

The success of the 'Mule' type of sheep has been gained at the expense of two other 'crosses'. The Masham, by the Teeswater or Wensleydale tup on the the the Dalesbred or Swaledale ewe; and the English Half-bred, by the Border Leicester tup on the Clun ewe. Other Half-breds, such as the Scotch and the Welsh, retain loyal supporters.

There is a host of other crosses, many well tried and successful and often developed for their ability to adapt to a particular region's climate or grazing. There have been several attempts to produce 'hybrid' sheep bred from a combination of crosses over many years and then establish a particular type able to breed true, i.e., if you mate two together the resultant lambs will be identical to both parents. Into this category comes the Cambridge, initially renowned for its ability to produce and rear anything up to five lambs. Pure Cambridge ewes seen suckling such large families are a fascinating sight but the commercial application of the breed is mainly through using a Cambridge ram as a crossing sire to lift lambing percentage in the progeny. If you had pure Texel ewes capable of 150 per cent lambing, by crossing them with a Cambridge your first-generation females could well lamb at over 200 per cent. This cross is now being increasingly tried and carries the unofficial tag 'Camtex'.The Colbred and the Meatlinc are two other hybrid sheep that have stood the test of time.

A Few Words of Advice

It is very difficult, well nigh impossible, for a book like this to recommend a particular breed. It would not only be unfair but also unwise. There are some breeds that are more popular than others among smallholders so it is well worth talking to others in similar circumstances to find out why they favour a certain breed or Halfbred. Smaller sheep can usually be stocked a bit tighter, allowing more to be kept per acre, and are easier to handle for routine tasks like foot-trimming and dosing.

Having said that, if you opt for a small rare breed you must ensure that fences and boundaries are escape-proof; although all fences used to contain sheep should be in good condition, some of the smaller rare breeds are adept at finding the smallest gap or even jumping a fence that a bigger breed would not tackle in normal circumstances. Consider a breed's breeding cycle and the time of year it lambs. The Down breeds like Suffolks and Hampshire Downs will lamb from December onwards, so if these take your fancy you will have to provide extra housing and be prepared for an increased workload in midwinter.

A Check-list

1. How much land is available?
2. Why do I want to keep sheep?
3. How much do I want to spend on stock?
4. How much time can I devote to running a flock?
5. What do I intend to do with surplus stock?
6. Do I need any extra training before I start?

A List of Breeds

Mountain and hill
Herdwick
Scottish Blackface
Swaledale
Cheviot
North Country Cheviot
Welsh Mountain
Derbyshire Gritstone
Lonk
Dalesbred
Whitefaced Woodland
Black Welsh Mountain
Rough Fell
Exmoor Horn
Brecknock Hill Cheviot
Hill Radnor
Welsh Hill Speckled-face
South Wales Mountain

Down
Suffolk
Hampshire Down
Dorset Down
Oxford
Southdown
Shropshire

Shortwool not Down
Clun
Ryeland
Kerry Hill
Hill Radnor
Beulah Speckled-face
Llanwenog
Wiltshire
Devon Closewool
Dorset Horn

Longwool
Wensleydale
Teeswater
Border Leicester
Blue-faced Leicester
Cotswold
Romney
Lincoln Longwool
Leicester Longwool
Devon Longwool

Primitive rare breeds
Hebridean
Manx Loghtan
Soay
Boreray
Castlemilk Moorit
Portland
North Ronaldsay

Other breeds
Jacob
Shetland

Imported breeds
Texel
Charollais
Bleu du Maine
Rouge de L'Ouest
Île de France
Berrichon du Cher
Merino
Charmoise
Vendeen
Beltex
Polwarth
Corriedale

The Continental Invasion

In the 1970s the British sheep industry was set for major change. The days of 'dog and stick' farming and the image of sheep production as the poor relation of other livestock enterprises were being replaced by improved management and increased profitability. With its huge range of native sheep breeds and crosses, few British farmers could see the advantages to be gained by importing even more breeds from Europe. But that is exactly what did happen and the impact on the UK sheep industry is still being felt. While the native Suffolk still retains top spot as the industry's leading sire of prime lambs for the commercial market, many of the continental sire breeds have now established themselves as major forces in this competitive market-place.

France was the initial source of the imported breeds and the Texel led the march. Like so many of the imported continentals, the Texel, with its origins in Holland, impressed British breeders with its shape. Its conformation had much to offer the prime lamb producer, having full and rounded hindquarters (gigots) and good fleshing. The breed's success at winter primestock shows has done much to enhance its reputation for producing high-quality carcass lambs. The Charollais was close on its heels and has established itself as a major force within the British sheep industry. This truly French import has a reputation for easy lambing and is widely used on hoggs where trouble-free lambing is a priority.

It is interesting here to linger on the word 'promotion', because the imported breeds launched elaborate promotional campaigns in the UK to win new customers from the sheep sector. And this they did. Never before had the British sheep industry seen such aggressive marketing of stock. But what it also achieved was to galvanize British breeds into action and many would agree that the improvement in our native breeds, primarily the Suffolk, has been a direct response to competition from continental breeders.

But gradually a host of new breeds began to arrive. The red-faced Rouge de L'Ouest and the blue-headed Bleu du Maine commanded huge prices in the early days and though their popularity has now 'settled', these breeds retain plenty of supporters. At one of the earliest sales of Bleu du Maine sheep in the mid- 1980s, over half a million pounds' worth of sheep were sold in one day at one market, such was the intensity of interest in these new breeds. The best Rouge de L'Ouest are well worthy of consideration by newcomers to sheep keeping; ewes are easy to lamb and lambs are quick to their feet and extremely active. These are traits common to most of the continental breeds though lambs often carry less wool than our native sheep and may need more protection in bad weather.

The white-faced Berrichon du Cher, a tall breed from France, and the Île de France have breed societies in the UK. The Roussin, a tough little French sheep, is well known for its hardiness, and the Beltex, a Belgian derivative of the Texel, is gaining ground for its extreme muscling. British Friesland arrived from Holland and have been widely used for cross-breeding as sheep dairying has increased in popularity in the UK.

British breeders continue to import new breeds. The Charmoise, looking something like a cross between a Charollais and a Texel, is an interesting prospect from France while the black-and-white Zwartbles (pronounced zwort-bless) from Holland is a big sheep that is very popular among smallholders in its native country. The Romanov from Russia has recently been imported into the UK from flocks in Europe; this sheep has the ability to breed out-of-season and is currently being evaluated in cross-breeding programmes with the aim of producing a hybrid.

Some British new faces have come from the southern hemisphere. The Merino originated in Spain but Australian and New Zealand stock has been imported. There are also the Polwarth and Corriedale breeds – both with Merino ancestry and produced primarily for their heavy fleeces of high-quality wool. There are various European versions of the Merino and the French-bred Est à Laine Merino, a most attractive sheep, has now been bred in the UK for several years.

Continental breeds and other imports will no doubt continue to arrive on British shores and each will endeavour to promote itself as being superior to any of its rivals. The promotion of continental breeds continues to be vigorous and several are worthy of close consideration by the small-scale sheep keeper. But look closely at each breed and check out the pros and cons. Whether the decision is taken to buy a native or a continental breed, the same evaluation criteria should be applied.

THREE

Grazing and Fencing

Grazing

The cheapest and most efficient way to feed a herbivore is with grass. A logical statement, you may think, but one that contains within it a degree of frustration for the small-scale sheep keeper who must learn to live with a 'feast or famine' scenario when it comes to growing grass. Most small flock owners are great 'jugglers' and while running even a few breeding ewes can often make life seem like a circus, I refer to the skill of juggling in the context of describing the skills necessary to learn to balance the availability of grass month-by-month, all year round. Running a small flock on a restricted acreage removes the degree of flexibility enjoyed by commercial sheep producers. Those who successfully breed and rear sheep on small acreages have to be good at what they do. Their mastery of husbandry techniques is often second to none and everyone develops their own way of 'juggling'. Even with a small amount of grazing, and assuming that you are going to buy in your winter stocks of hay, it helps if you can divide the grassland area by restricting sheep to 'paddocks'. By splitting land in this way you go some way to achieving your own style of the flexibility enjoyed by those who run ewes on hundreds of acres. Dividing land in this way will enable you to keep it fresh and sweet for ewes and lambs in spring and to have enough 'bite' in the autumn for tupping. And remember that if these paddocks are adjacent and accessed by a gate or split by electric fencing there is no reason why the whole area cannot be opened up if necessary.

Worm infestation is the biggest threat to sheep and the longer sheep graze the same land, the higher the risk. The system of 'clean grazing' is widely practised commercially but can be difficult to undertake where the land acreage is limited. It involves rotating sheep around a block of land and alternating grazing with cattle so that ewes and lambs begin the season on land that was grazed by cattle the previous year. The 'clean' grass on which the flock is grazed is free from worm eggs and, in theory, will create a flock that will not become infested with worms.

This is a luxury open to few small-flock owners; a strict programme of drenching lambs every three weeks throughout the grazing season and treating ewes before and after lambing must be followed where land is used continuously for sheep.

Do not assume that a piece of rough land that has not been ploughed within living memory and appears to lack the green sward effect you would like is automatically unsuitable. Hopefully, you will have selected a breed or type of sheep to suit your geographical location and sheep can often transform a most unprepossessing piece of ground into a respectable pasture. But much will depend on the breed, so take advice.

It may be that you do decide to plough and re-seed either all or part of your land. Your best option is to contact a local agricultural contractor to undertake the job; striking up a relationship here will be useful. There will be other times of the year when his skills, like using the chain-harrows to drag out all the dead grass from the sward in early spring, will be needed. If this is your first venture into stock keeping, you will find that you soon establish a good rapport with your local agricultural merchant. When it comes to selecting seed for your new pasture, he should be able to put you in touch with the local representative from a grass-seed company who will advise on whether to go for a long- or short-term ley – ley referring to the pasture. A long-term ley is advisable, but you will need to take advice on the grass species most suited to your land and needs, and on what level of clover should be included. Clover is a useful constituent of any grass-seed mixture and will 'fix' nitrogen from the air, thus benefiting the entire sward.

It is very difficult to be specific about how many sheep you can keep to the acre. So many factors are involved – breed of sheep, location, type of land (heavy or light), how well drained the land is, rainfall, condition of the sward and whether you are able to house the flock for part of the winter. We are back to 'juggling' again, because many small-flock owners admit that they keep too many sheep on their limited acres. What is a source of constant amazement is how well they do it despite these limitations.

The stocking rate – the number of sheep you can keep per acre – must also take account of lambs; when you consider that many ewes have twins and a proportion will produce even triplets, the stock you are carrying in summer could increase by threefold or more compared with your winter flock size. It is obvious that you would not be able to keep as many Hampshire Downs as Manx Loghtans on the same piece of ground simply because the sheer size difference increases the feed demand of the larger breed. Stocking rates can vary from 8.3 ewes per hectare to 15 ewes per hectare, including lambs, and is dependent on the variables listed above. For guidance, it is better to stock on the low side to start with and go through a full year: if you have spare grazing capacity, it is never too difficult to buy in some extra sheep just to tide you over. Winter is really the testing time and no flock should be established at what is considered to be full capacity until it has the experience of a full winter's management.

When trying to estimate how much winter feed you will have to buy in, a useful guide is to reckon a ewe will eat about 0.45 kg of hay a day from December to March, although this will vary widely from breed to breed.

Weed control over a small acreage is often more easily done by hand if nettles or docks are a problem. Herbicides are an option if the problem is severe, but take advice. There are now strict rules concerning the use of agro-chemicals, so it may be worth contacting an agricultural contractor to do the job for you. It is likely that you will need to call on him in spring and autumn to apply nitrogenous fertilizer to improve grass output. It may seem a luxury but spreading fertilizer must be done correctly; attempting to apply it by hand from a wheelbarrow will only lead to uneven distribution and possible scorching of the grass where too many of the fertilizer pellets are deposited. Phosphate and potash will also be needed by the growing sward but you would be well advised to seek guidance from either a local farmer or a fertilizer company representative. Local knowledge is a great base from which to start, but soil sampling will give a profile of your grassland's requirements. Increasingly popular among owners of small acreages is fertilizer based on seaweed which may not produce a heavy grass crop following nitrogenous fertilizer applications but will encourage sustained development of the sward. Stock grazed on land treated with this material are widely considered to show improved growth rates and general health and vigour.

Springtime will not only provide the lushest grazing of the year but also the most nutritious. Although this is invaluable at a time when lactating ewes need to reach 'peak performance' and maintain it, ewes and lambs impose their greatest demands on grassland during the summer as lambs' dependency on milk diminishes and more forage is taken. But a dry summer can pose difficulties for the small-flock owner and there should be no hesitation in supplying additional hay if conditions are extremely dry and stock is clearly not able to sustain itself from grazing alone. Autumn grass, particularly after a dry summer, can look plentiful and spring-like, but beware. Nutritionally, autumn grass looks much better than it really is, which is why it is often termed 'green water'. Do not be reluctant to put out some straw in racks or even hay at this time of year.

Fencing

The best grazing in the world is no use to any flock that cannot be contained upon it. And you can be sure that no matter how good your own pasture is, any opportunity to escape into the field next door, even though it may be full of docks and weeds, will never be missed by any self-respecting sheep. There is nothing more attractive to look at, more protective towards sheep and of more value to wildlife than a thick hawthorn or mixed boundary hedge. If you have fields dissected by hedges you should consider yourself fortunate and everything should be done to maintain them. Although these boundaries may have previously contained horses or cattle, they will not always be stockproof to sheep. Hedges under consideration as an effective boundary must be thoroughly checked; gaps must be dealt with using sheep netting and stakes and ideally planted up with young hedging which will eventually 'plug' the gap permanently. A very 'gappy' hedge may well require a fence to be erected along its entire length. Electric fencing systems are now widely available for sheep and can be extremely useful in managing a few acres of grassland. They run off a battery-operated fencer unit and provide a flexible method of controlling your flock's grazing. On your travels, you will no doubt see a wide variety of items and materials used for fencing. Small-scale sheep keepers are nothing if not inventive when it comes to keeping their sheep where they want them. But wire bread-trays and bedsteads, boxes and chicken crates are not only unsightly but also totally ineffective in providing a barrier. The most widely used fencing for sheep, certainly for all boundary fences, comprises wooden posts and sheep netting to which a strand of barbed wire can be added at the top for additional height. The key to achieving a sound and long-lasting fence is the distance between the posts and the tension achieved on the wire via the strainer posts positioned at the end of each straight line of fencing. It isn't difficult to master the art of fencing, but I would advise anyone considering tackling their own for the first time to contact a local farmer for a few tips or even your local agricultural college or ATB Landbase to enquire about fencing courses. Fencing materials are not cheap so it is worthwhile ensuring that your investment is put to the best use. Alternatively you can call on the services of an agricultural fencer who will recommend the style and type of fencing you need. If you have undulating land or ground that is a far cry from the flat, level fields most fencers dream of, this is an option I would strongly advocate. Consider where best to position access gates and whether you may at some stage need to gain entry with a tractor – in other words, err on the side of larger rather than smaller.

Your fencing man may also be able to provide you with a simple 'funnel' system or an even more elaborate in-field handling arrangement for catching and dealing with the flock. Sheep can be the most frustrating animals to catch and move around, but a simple system that will funnel them into a field corner and provide one or two pens and an exit gate will eliminate hours of wasted time and stress for both you and your sheep. It is sheer joy to see sheep run up the tailgate and into a trailer without any physical intervention when the norm has been a sweated brow and aching back after a laborious session manhandling uncooperative sheep.

FOUR

Housing

*To House or Not to House – The Advantages and Disadvantages of
Keeping Sheep Inside – Makeshift Shelters – Space Allocation for Ewes
– Trough Space Requirements – Siting Your Building – The
Importance of Ventilation – Sheep-house Floors – Sheep-house
Dimensions – Ewe and Lamb Verandah*

The first question to ask yourself about providing housing for
your sheep flock is, 'Do I really need it?' The answer is probably
no, but that is not to say that a lot of newcomers to keeping sheep
do not put up a sheep shed. If you have decided to lamb pedigree
sheep in midwinter – say, breeds such as Suffolk, Charollais or
even commercial cross-bred ewes – then you will definitely need
a building in which to house your sheep before, during and after
lambing. But do not assume that a traditional spring-lambing
flock does not require any housing. Perhaps you are beginning to
understand how arbitrary the question of housing sheep really
can be.

There were times not long ago when putting sheep in a building was unheard of. The shepherds of old, even those lambing in
winter, would erect temporary shelters to lamb the flock close to
the farm. In southern England, wattle-hurdles were used to 'fold'
or graze ewes and lambs, often on fields of turnips or other winter roots. These dedicated flockmasters would find it difficult to
justify the elaborate and hugely expensive indoor sheep systems
that many commercial farms have today. And it is not just lowland flocks. Many hill sheep are now housed for part of the winter even though they do not lamb until April. Why?, you may ask.
The answer has nothing to do with the type of sheep or their
lambing date but the decision to bring sheep under cover for part
of the winter is a calculated management tactic. The newcomer to
sheep keeping should sit down and make a similar assessment

when involved in his own deliberations concerning a sheep house.

To bring sheep inside during part of the winter does have its advantages. For the small-scale flock owner, land may be limited. To take ewes off grazing pasture in the winter will give the land a valuable rest, prevent the ground becoming poached (muddy) and allow a valuable bite of spring grass in fields that have been well rested during the winter. And for the shepherd who has to spend time away from home each day, it is heartening to know that your flock is safely under cover – no more wandering round the field in the pitch dark trying to count sheep and grappling with a feed-trough in moonlight while the flock is hell-bent on bringing you to your knees!

Having sheep inside during the bleakest and coldest months of the year is the most convenient way to run a flock from the shepherd's point of view, but there are also advantages for the sheep. Improved utilization of feed will be achieved when ewes are indoors; you will have more time to stand and stare even if it is late at night – something you cannot do with a flock at grass in the winter. Ewe condition can be more closely monitored and hay wastage is minimized. Undoubtedly the biggest advantage of housing ewes in the winter comes at lambing-time. By bringing ewes indoors several weeks before lambing, you are able to keep a close eye on ewe condition, easily spot any ewes that are not feeding or are unwell and generally perform management tasks less stressfully and more efficiently. If you decide to house your flock during the winter you do not necessarily have to keep sheep inside for months on end. It may be that you have ample grazing and that your land is free-draining or that you simply prefer to leave your sheep at grass until, say, two weeks before lambing. In this situation you could use the accommodation just to make lambing-time more convenient and turn ewes out with their lambs within forty-eight hours of being born. And remember that if you do have a building you can always make use of it in a host of other ways when the sheep are not inside, so a building is never wasted if you are running a flock of sheep.

But now let us look at the other side of the argument and

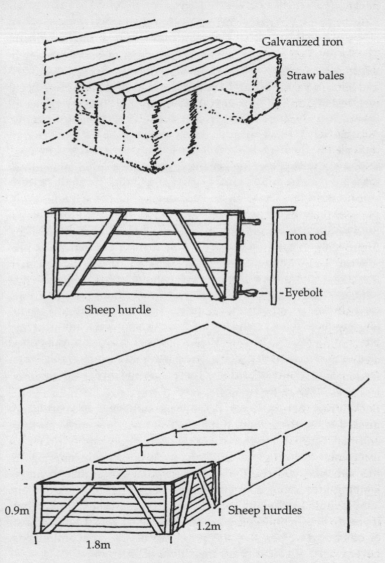

Galvanized iron

Straw bales

Iron rod

Eyebolt

Sheep hurdle

0.9m

1.8m

1.2m

Sheep hurdles

Figure 6. Simple outdoor and indoor pens

33

assume that you do not have any existing buildings and that you feel more inclined to invest in sheep than in concrete and timber. Let me make it quite clear: you can successfully run a flock of sheep without having an elaborate house to keep them in during the winter, providing you take several things into consideration. Make sure you are not overstocked; remember that those lush summer pastures will not support the same number of sheep in the bare and wet months of winter and though you may appear to have plenty of grass in September it will be a very different picture by November. Hay and silage can always be fed to ewes kept outside but the biggest danger caused by overstocking in winter is damage to the land; the last thing you want is a sun-baked mud bath left over from the winter struggling to turn itself into a fresh spring pasture. A ewe flock kept outside in the winter should have some form of shelter and by that I mean a good thick hedge to stand up against prevailing winds or even shelter afforded by the side of an adjacent building. Healthy, well-fed and carefully managed sheep should out-winter perfectly happily. If you have no building you should make sure you have a handling area at one corner of the field. A few wooden sheep hurdles, fence posts and a roll of sheep netting can be imaginatively combined to create a 'funnel' into which sheep can be driven when any management tasks need to be performed. The last thing you must do is start chasing in-lamb ewes around the field in midwinter when you need to foot-trim or dose. These jobs, and any vet checks, can be undertaken in the handling area.

Lambing-time without a building can have its frustrating moments but straw bales are marvellous for stacking together to create temporary sheep shelters and pens. Be adventurous with a few sheets of corrugated tin and you can create temporary, low-cost 'in-field' housing that will at least give cover for ewes and lambs for the first day or so after lambing.

On your travels you will see some very impressive 'sheep palaces' that have been built as commercial sheep farming has become more profitable in recent years. The small-scale flock owner must not think such structures are a prerequisite of good flock management. If you choose your breed carefully to suit your circumstances and the grazing you have available, you can successfully run a 'fresh-air-flock' equally as well as those who choose to bring their sheep inside.

Sheep-house Considerations

If you decide to invest in a sheep house or opt to convert an existing building, there are one or two factors that must remain uppermost in your mind. Ventilation is absolutely critical. A sheep house must not be draughty but it must have adequate ventilation. Unlike humans, who come indoors to keep warm, heat is the last thing a sheep needs from its accommodation. Shelter from the worst of the weather is the aim and any new or converted building and the design must make adequate allowance for a free flow of air at all times. If you are in any doubt about this, you should seek expert advice from an experienced sheep keeper, or your vet may advise. Failure to achieve adequate ventilation will lead to airborne diseases thriving in a warm and muggy atmosphere, leading to a host of health problems in your flock.

The other important aspect of the house is the floor. Sheep kept inside tend to be more prone to foot problems; to avoid them, it is important to create a free-draining base to the house if you are starting from scratch. If you have a building with an existing solid floor you must make sure there is a deep bed of straw which is regularly replenished to provide sheep with an upper surface of clean, dry material. If it is a new shed, site it away from prevailing winds and remember that you will need to have power installed, so the closer you can build it to existing services the cheaper the exercise will be. Before housing them, it is always wise to check the flock's feet thoroughly and to run ewes through a foot bath. Remember that sheep should only be brought inside on a dry day. Housing sheep with wet fleeces is asking for trouble.

Some Housing Ideas

The pole-barn is probably the cheapest way to provide housing for sheep. Old telegraph poles and corrugated tin can be used to construct this basic accommodation. The back and sides need to be sheeted but the front – at about 8 ft (2.5 m) high, running to 6 ft (2 m) high at the back – can be left open. This type of house needs to be in a sheltered spot to avoid wind constantly blowing in through the open front and bedding costs can be high, but it is better than nothing if you have to bring sheep off the land in winter.

A slightly more elaborate mono-pitch house can be constructed of timber, basing its size on a space requirement per ewe of around three metres square, although for smaller and rare primitive breeds this can be reduced. The back and sides should be timber-framed and the roof can either be of tin or some of the new sheeted roofing materials now available. Approximate dimensions could be 20 ft x 16 ft (6 m x 5 m) standing 8 ft (2.5 m) at the front and running to 6 ft (2 m) at the rear. There should be adequate air-flow via vents in the back wall of the shed and the design of the front should provide the shepherd with further control of the building's ventilation. A little under half the front could be fitted with Yorkshire-boarding – timber boards nailed on from roof to floor leaving a 20 mm gap in between. Access is an important feature of any building, so do not make it difficult for yourself or your sheep. You will be making regular trips in and out of the shed, so hang a three-foot 'paddock' gate at one end. Next to that, remembering that you may have to get inside with a machine to muck-out and also that sheep are easier to drive through a wide opening than a narrow one, hang a ten-foot farm gate. The open area above the gates can be left to achieve a healthy atmosphere if the building has been correctly sited, but weather changes and freak winter snowstorms can cause chaos if allowed to drive into the open front of this type of building. It may therefore be worth considering investing in a fail-safe by fitting some heavy-duty Netlon plastic netting above the open space at the front. If you really want to push the boat out, this can now be purchased as 'roller blinds' so that it can be pulled into position quickly if bad weather strikes. Whatever arrangements you choose, always remember that ventilation is extremely important. A cold morning can turn into a very warm afternoon in early spring and inside a shed full of sheep a sudden rise in temperature can be dangerous. Always err of the side of keeping your sheep cool. It is better to let the wool on their backs regulate their temperature: it has been doing it a lot longer than we have.

Inside the building you need to provide a hay-rack and a feed-trough. Allow 10–12 ft (3–4 m) of trough space to enable sheep to feed without competition driving shy feeders away. Hay-racks can be bought, or home-made affairs constructed using sheep netting and timber. A word of warning for those with horses who venture into sheep keeping: if you have horned sheep, do not use hay-nets. Horned breeds can easily get caught in them and have been known to hang themselves. Always make sure sheep have adequate clean water. Sheep that seemed to drink very little at grass will double or treble their intake when switched to a predominantly hay diet. I get concerned about heavily in-lamb ewes jostling at the trough. The whole business of getting feed into the trough around a mass of ravenous ewes can prove difficult. It may be worth making an arrangement at the front of the building so that the trough can be filled from the outside, thus avoiding the stampede.

A 'hard-standing' area, constructed of crushed stone or road-planings and fenced off in front of the building, provided our January-lambing ewes and lambs with a welcome exercise area on kinder days of midwinter weather. Where land is still too wet to turn sheep out but it is clear that the confines of the shed are proving rather restrictive, such an outside area can prove a great boon to a flock. The added space outside the house is also welcome as lambs start to grow, and it prevents ewes becoming 'stale' after being inside for several weeks.

Innovation is the key to any form of sheep housing or shelter but remember that your stock must have adequate ventilation and that their feet must be kept dry.

FIVE

Feeding and Nutrition

*When to Feed – Feeding the Ewe at Tupping Time – Pre-lambing
Dietary Needs – Feeding Hay – Roots for Winter Feed – Molasses –
Coarse Mixes Versus Concentrates – Feeding for Milk Yield – Creep
Feeding Lambs – Mineral Needs*

Providing a sheep can graze and there is ample grass to sustain it,
the need for supplementary feeding in terms of concentrates or
cereals is minimal. That statement is broadly true although there
are exceptions. If you are running a small flock of sheep as a
hobby, or a breed that will outwinter and lamb in March to April,
your management will be straightforward. The level of nutrition
will have to be increased prior to and during tupping and again
during the final six weeks of pregnancy, assuming that through
the winter months your flock has adequate grazing and additional hay when necessary. For breeds like the Charollais and the
Suffolk, which are tupped in July and August, to lamb indoors in
midwinter, the problem is keeping weight off the ewes as they
gain condition off good summer grass. These breeds, and others
with a similar breeding cycle, do not need any extra feed at tupping time. Other breeds that lamb in spring may well be suckling
lambs into late summer. These, and particularly older ewes of this
type, can lose body condition quickly in late lactation, a situation
which is accentuated by the reduced nutritional value of grazing
at this time of year. It is these breeds that need to be looked at
carefully at weaning and any ewes which are clearly 'light' in condition must either be fed extra 'hard' feed or moved on to good
grazing for several weeks prior to tupping. If your small flock is
being tupped in the autumn I think it can be useful to offer about
0.25 kg per head per day of a coarse sheep mix about two weeks
before the tup goes in, increasing to about 0.5 kg and then gradually tailing off towards Christmas. I believe this is enough to

maintain the correct level of nutrition for the ewe without risk of her becoming over-fat which can lead to low levels of conception. By feeding ewes each day, you also have an easy job of checking the flock at the trough; though take care not to make too much fuss of the tup: they are his ewes and even the best-tempered tups can sometimes resent any disturbance, however well meaning. My own experience of feeding at this time of year has always produced healthy ewes and strong, vigorous lambs. Even ewe hoggs, taking the tup in their first year, usually produce a lamb on this system and cope perfectly well as young mothers.

If grazing is limited, you should ensure newly tupped ewes have access to additional fodder in the form of hay in a hay-rack. Wheeled racks are ideal and can be moved around as the area close by becomes muddy; alternatively, home-made wooden racks can easily be built and allowed to free-stand or hung on a wall. Some innovative ideas for feeding hay will often be seen. Of the best is the system of slinging chicken wire between posts to form a hammock-effect which provides sheep with a feed-face at both sides. The only problem can arise when horned sheep are being fed and inadvertently get their horns stuck in the wire, so this is a system that must be considered carefully if you are unable to check your flock regularly. Hay should always be fed ad lib. Buy the best hay you can, free from dust and mould. Do not be afraid to ask the person you are buying it from to split a bale so you can have a good look inside. Try to buy hay made that season and ask around for good suppliers: good haymakers are worth getting to know if you want to have healthy sheep. Remember not to feed hay on the ground and to protect racks from the rain. Sheep will not eat wet hay. Turnips and swedes are another useful supplement for winter feeding. Some feed them as chopped roots; others prefer to lay a few whole ones out in the field for the sheep to eat at their leisure. Whenever hay is being fed, water intake will increase markedly; but whatever winter diet you select, always ensure fresh, clean water is available.

What to Feed

There are many options, including compound feeds in the form of concentrate pellets, coarse mix, feed blocks, sugar-beet pulp or pellets, and cereal grains. I am a great advocate of a mixed ration for sheep. Although compound pellets are professionally formulated to contain everything the sheep needs in its diet, I have always preferred to feed a mix. These coarse rations are made by all feed companies and comprise a combination of grains and cereals, and can be bought with or without added molasses. But the major feed compounders have always erred on the side of the concentrate pellet for their in-lamb rations until recently. Now, thankfully, there are feed compounders who can offer higher protein percentage diets in the form of a coarse mix. For pre-lambing nutrition, a ewe needs to start receiving extra feed about six weeks before she lambs. Start with about 0.25 kg a day and build up over the next four weeks to 1 kg, although a small ewe like a Shetland or Black Welsh Mountain will need a little less than a kilo. When commercial farmers have hundreds of sheep to feed each day, there is no way they can guarantee exactly how much every ewe is eating. Small-flock owners can be more diligent, but talk to others who keep the same breed and find out what works best for them. Feeding sheep can be a very inexact science, but you will soon learn to know whether your sheep are getting too much or too little. For spring-lambing ewes I continue to feed outside for several weeks, well into May if the spring is late. This is the time when your lambs will be growing. You will never be able to put anything in their mouths in their entire lifetime that will nourish them more than their mother's milk, so it is time and money well spent making sure that the lactating ewe is fed well enough to keep the milk flowing.

It is much safer to feed a readily prepared ration in preference to offering cereals such as barley and oats. These must be fed as part of a balanced diet and if you are determined to feed these grains you must have a diet professionally formulated. Other options include sugar-beet shreds – an excellent source of energy – which many sheep keepers prefer to soak for several hours before feeding, although it can also be safely fed dry; and raw molasses in self-lick ball feeders can be another useful source of energy. Some farmers have successfully relied on giving molasses in this way instead of any concentrate feeding as a way of reducing feed costs but for the small-flock owner I would consider molasses as an additional feed and not as an alternative.

If you decide to show your sheep, you will have to feed them to achieve the correct amount of 'condition'. There are various mixes, many of them handed down through generations of shepherds, that are tried and tested to do the job. Talk to fellow breeders and exhibitors and try to pick up a few tips, but remember that the secret is to get your sheep fit and not fat. Whole barley is often a major component of these show-conditioning mixes but the novice sheep keeper must be aware that overfeeding barley can kill sheep. Cabbages fed whole are an excellent way to put condition on sheep for the showring.

Creep feeding is always a topic of much debate among shepherds. Early lambing flocks – pedigree or commercial – always offer creep feed to their lambs about ten days after birth. These highly palatable tiny pellets, which should contain a coccidiostat for lambs kept indoors, will encourage dry-feed intake from an early age. Specially designed creep feeders are available, or an area of the building can be sectioned off using posts arranged so that they allow small lambs through and keep the ewes out. The feed can gradually be switched to a coarse lamb mix if feeding is to continue when the lambs are turned out, but much will depend on the breed and whether your intentions are to produce an early prime lamb for slaughter or are aiming at the summer sales of pedigree sheep like Suffolk, Texel and Charollais. Although the majority of those who keep these three major breeds all offer creep feed to baby lambs, there are some who have resisted and allowed the ewes to do the job. Many have been surprised at how well lambs have fared off mothers' milk alone, assuming that the compensatory growth rate is due to the lambs demanding more milk and the ability of well-fed ewes to respond by producing it. The whole issue of creep feeding is a complex one and you will have to decide for yourself if you consider it worthwhile.

Dietary needs also encompass the mineral requirements of sheep. Always have a mineral 'lick' on offer. They are available from all farm stores and should be given to sheep both inside and at grass. It may be useful to take soil and blood samples to check what deficiencies your flock may be most vulnerable to.

Always keep feeding utensils clean and in winter always turn troughs over after each feed, to ensure they remain clean and dry. Move troughs around the field to avoid one area becoming a mud-bath in wet weather.

Most sheep will eat until they are ill so do not be tempted to overfeed. Even in the hardest of winter weather, a rack full of top-quality hay will be the sheep's lifeline, especially if it is positioned well away from driving wind and rain.

SIX

Preparing for Lambing

Lambing Seasons – Breed Options – Gestation – Flushing –
Condition Scoring – Ewe Foot Check – Udder Lumps – Worming –
Clostridial Vaccinations – Management Pre-tupping – Ram-check and
Pre-tupping Care – Raddling and Harnesses – Feeding in Early
Pregnancy

There is nothing quite so rejuvenating as the sight of new-born lambs leaping and skipping with the sheer love of life itself. Their *joie de vivre* is a symbol of winter's passing and heralds the season of rebirth and vitality in the country calendar. And yet 'the lambing', as it is referred to, is not strictly confined to springtime. The breeding cycle of most sheep is directly influenced by the hours of daylight. Among the indigenous hill breeds, such as the Herdwick, Swaledale and Scottish Blackface, a hormonal change is triggered as the days shorten, leading to the onset of oestrus – the time when ewes are in breeding condition. Primitive rare breeds such as the Hebridean, Boreray and Soay also fall into this category of traditional late autumn breeders. And it is not difficult to understand why. Many of these breeds have evolved with little interference from man and the demands of modern farming. There would be little point in their producing lambs any earlier than the true onset of spring in late March or April. So these breeds have a natural breeding cycle which ensures their lambs are only born when the weather is kind enough to ensure maximum survival and spring grass is coming through to keep the ewe's milk flowing.

Particularly among small-scale sheep keepers, it is not uncommon to find sheep successfully kept on land that is a far cry from their natural environment. The stoic gaze of a grey-fleeced Herdwick standing to face a fell-blown gale or the independent air of a majestic Rough Fell ram have all too often won the hearts

43

of those whose grazings are not only kinder but more limited than the mountainous expanses these sheep are more used to. In less extreme climes and with the higher level of nutrition this affords, it may be possible for these breeds to 'take the tup' a little earlier, though nothing is guaranteed with such truly indigenous sheep.

The heavy down breeds, such as Suffolks, Shropshires and Hampshire Downs, and many of the imports such as Charollais and Vendeen, will start to ovulate from midsummer. These are among the earliest of lambing breeds and those running pedigree flocks will be busy in the lambing shed from early December, with the aim of having lambs well grown by turnout in the spring and the intention of selling rams as breeding stock at the special breed society sales which start in midsummer.

The Dorset Horn and Dorset Down breeds are also renowned for their ability to breed 'out-of-season' and will take the tup at virtually any time of the year. This has a big advantage for commercial farmers who can make the most of this trait by producing three crops of lambs in two years. For the small-scale sheep keeper, the ability of these breeds to conceive so readily can be a drawback unless strict control measures are in place to monitor tups and ensure lambs are born when *you* want them. Commercial lowland breeds such as the North of England Mule, the Welsh Mule and the Welsh Half-bred will lamb as early as January in some cases, though conception rates are not as high at this time of year. If the intention is to produce an early crop of lambs from these prolific and well-proven commercial crossbreds, oestrus can be induced by using hormone-impregnated sponges inserted into the ewe's vagina. Your veterinary surgeon can advise on 'spongeing' and artificial insemination, which can be useful breeding aids in a small flock by affording total control over the lambing date, although consideration must be given to the costs involved.

The gestation period of all sheep is 147–151 days – around five months – with females becoming sexually mature at anything from six to eight months. Ewes ovulate for one to two days and will come into season every sixteen days. The pros and cons of 'flushing' ewes prior to tupping is one of the most hotly debated topics among sheep farmers.

Flushing refers to providing ewes with an improved level of nutrition in the weeks running up to mating with the intention of increasing the number of eggs being shed by the ewe, leading to a high conception rate and hopefully a high percentage of twin births. A move to fresh pasture is the most widely practised method, though for those with limited acres there is the option of introducing extra-concentrated feeding to achieve the same result. The golden rule is to remember that the fatter the sheep the less likely she is to conceive and even if she does she may only produce one lamb, whereas in the correct condition she could have produced twins or even triplets.

Many experienced sheep farmers judge pre-tupping condition of their ewes by 'eye', but that is not to say they always get it right. To improve this judgement, a system known as 'condition scoring' is now widely practised and is well worth mastering to ensure your flock is carrying exactly the correct amount of 'flesh' before the tup is turned in. Condition scoring is based upon feeling the fat and muscle cover along the backbone of the sheep. With practice, the varying body condition of sheep that are either too thin or too fat can be assessed using the fingers to determine how much 'cover' there is over the vertical and horizontal processes of a sheep's backbone. The actual score ranges from 0 to 5 and is used to indicate just how fat or thin a sheep is.

Score 0. This is seldom used. No muscle or fatty tissue can be felt; the animal would be extremely emaciated and on the point of death.

Score 1. There is a sharpness and pointedness to the horizontal processes. It is easy to push fingers below the horizontals and each process can be felt. The loin muscle is thin and with no fat cover.

Score 2. Individual processes can only be felt as corrugations. They are prominent but smooth to the touch, although it is still possible to press the fingers underneath. The loin muscle is of moderate depth but with little fat cover.

Score 3. The vertical processes are smooth and rounded and the bone can only be felt with pressure. The horizontal processes are smooth and well covered and hard pressure with the fingers is needed to locate the ends. The loin muscle is full and has moderate fat cover.

Score 4. The vertical processes are only detectable as a line; the ends of the horizontal processes cannot be felt. The loin muscles are full and have a thick covering of fat.

Score 5. The vertical processes cannot be detected even when pressure is applied. There is a dimple in the fat layers where the processes should be. The horizontal processes cannot be detected and the loin muscles are very full and covered with very thick fat.

Condition scoring of ewes, after weaning or at the latest eight weeks before tupping, is a critical management check, the value of which cannot be overestimated. Sufficient time is needed to correct the condition of ewes prior to tupping. Extensive research by ADAS (Agriculture and Development Advisory Service) sheep specialists has shown that the condition of ewes has a direct bearing on their lambing percentage and their health during pregnancy. Thin ewes (below condition score 2) and fat ewes (above condition score 4) will never perform to their full potential. Ewes in poor condition during pregnancy are more at risk from pregnancy toxaemia (twin-lamb disease), will produce weak lambs and have insufficient yields of all-important colostrum for their lambs; fat ewes are more likely to suffer from vaginal prolapse, especially those fed ad lib roughage, and are more prone to lambing problems.

Never forget that it takes at least eight weeks to alter the condition score by one point. The most effective way of achieving such modifications is by managing grazing according to condition.

Small-scale sheep keepers are most likely to opt for a traditional spring lambing, but looking ahead to a successful crop of lambs means planning must start in the autumn. Once the ewes are running with the ram it is better to interfere with the flock as little as possible.

Daily feeding will obviously have to be undertaken but it is advisable to have completed any other stock-management tasks well in advance.

Sheep are renowned for their foot problems; while some breeds have good, hard feet and suffer little – usually the hill and mountain breeds – others require regular attention. The whole subject of lame sheep is becoming a major animal welfare issue. Despite the fact that many farmers adopt a strict programme of foot treatment, they still have lame ewes, a problem which can be extremely frustrating. Owners of small flocks would be well advised to be rigorous over the monitoring of their ewes' feet and particularly before tupping time. A ewe in pain because of foot-rot, scald, or one of the host of problems that can attack a sheep's feet is more likely to have her oestrus cycle affected and be less likely to mate readily, which will affect her breeding potential. So a few weeks before tupping, the feet of the entire flock should be checked; excessive horn growth should be pared and the ewes allowed to walk slowly through a foot bath. This topic is dealt with more fully in the chapter on sheep health.

At the pre-tupping check, it may also be worth 'dagging' the ewes. This refers to clipping out excess wool around the hindquarters, and removing any dirty fleece, which may interfere with mating. This opportunity of looking through the flock should also be used to check ewes' teeth and udders. You will often see sheep advertised using the terminology 'correct above and below', referring to ewes having a full set of teeth and being free from any udder problems. This should ensure that ewes have the correct dentition to enable them to graze and adequately meet their dietary needs, and have udders without blind teats, mastitic lumps or other disorders that may impede lactation. Owners of small flocks may well decide to retain certain sheep for sentimental or other reasons, whereas a commercial enterprise has a more demanding criteria and tends to cull 'problem' ewes. The level of individual shepherding to be found among smaller-flock owners can successfully support a ewe demanding more care.

Teeth need to be examined closely. Decisions must be taken about ewes showing premature loss of incisor teeth which can affect their feed intake during pregnancy. That is not to say that 'broken-mouthed' ewes will not thrive, far from it. Many 'old girls' can be nursed for years and successfully rear lambs, but a shepherd needs to know that the young ewe with a full set of teeth is going to find life a lot easier during the winter than a senior citizen with only gums to suck up the grass. Most ewes keep their incisor teeth until they are five or six years old and examination of a sheep's mouth can be used to determine its age. If ewes are being bought in to supplement a breeding flock, it is advisable to open a ewe's mouth and check her age for yourself.

Ewes already in the flock and any that are bought in should always have their udders checked. Any lumps suggest a ewe has suffered from mastitis; some ewes cope with mastitis during lac-

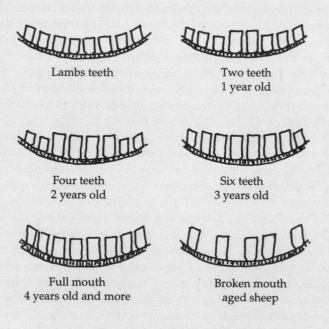

Lambs teeth

Two teeth
1 year old

Four teeth
2 years old

Six teeth
3 years old

Full mouth
4 years old and more

Broken mouth
aged sheep

Figure 7. Dentition of sheep

tation without the shepherd realizing there is a problem. The milk from the infected part of the udder dries up and after weaning the mastitis can leave 'lumpy tissue'. It may be useful to mention here that sheep breeders refer to teats as 'quarters' even though the normal number of teats is two – no doubt a carry over from the dairy industry. Mastitis during lactation can render the infected quarter useless in future years, but that is not to say that the ewe is unfit to breed from, unless both quarters are affected.

It can be very frustrating for a new-born lamb to keep sucking at a non-functional teat when the other is full of milk; in the first few days, lambs suckling ewes with one quarter need careful watching. The penny usually drops in time. A good ewe with twins may well be able to rear both her offspring even if she only has one quarter; although it is wise to keep a close eye on the family to make sure one lamb does not start to lose out on the milk bar. Never leave a ewe with one quarter without any lambs. The old shepherds say this is a sure way to 'poison' the other teat. Pedigree flocks with senior ewes of proven breeding ability may prefer to retain sheep that are unable to rear their own lambs. This does add to the workload at lambing-time and it is possible that retaining females from ewes that have shown a tendency to mastitis may lead to the problem being perpetuated in the flock in future years.

So, having ensured that your ewes are sound on their feet, are carrying the right amount of condition, can be easily mated and look likely to survive the winter and suckle their lambs, the next job is to worm the entire flock.

It is important to note here that if any ewe lambs are being introduced into the flock for breeding in their first year they must receive a clostridial injection in the autumn prior to tupping. Bought-in ewes which are already on the clostridial vaccine system and have received the necessary two injections in the first few months of life need only receive a booster jab each year, about six weeks before lambing. If space allows, newly bought-in sheep can be isolated from the main flock for about two weeks to ensure they are fit and healthy and unlikely to infect the existing flock.

About three weeks before the ram is introduced to the ewes, it is advisable to 'flush' the flock. This term refers to introducing the ewes to a rising plane of nutrition and helps the ovaries to shed more eggs and hopefully increase the number of lambs born. Flushing is best achieved by moving ewes to new pasture, but for those on a limited acreage the feed bag is a useful aid. Even if you have only a small area of ground it can be of great benefit if you can close some of it off before tupping time. Ewes given a fresh 'bite' of grass with some additional concentrate feeding usually show their thanks five months later.

Down breeds, taking the ram in midsummer, do not need to be flushed. One of the biggest headaches is keeping weight off these ewes, which thrive on good summer grazing. For ewes tupped in the autumn, it is worth feeding 0.25 kg per day of a coarse ration for two to three weeks before tupping and continuing this for three weeks afterwards. If grass is short and winter sets in early, it may be advisable to continue feeding well into December. Foetal reabsorption can be a problem if nutrition levels decline after mating. With small flocks, it is better to be safe than sorry.

Ewes come on heat or cycle every sixteen days and remain receptive to mating for 24–48 hours. There are many schools of thought on whether or not to mate ewe lambs in their first year. It is not usual to have a crop of lambs from breeds like Suffolks and Hampshire Downs before they are a year old, though there are exceptions. Most commercial hill flocks of Swaledales, Herdwick or Scottish Blackface would not be mated in their first season and would be allowed to grow and develop in readiness for taking the tup as shearlings.

Many small-scale sheep keepers with primitive breeds usually follow the same principle, although from personal experience I have found that well-grown primitive females will successfully take the tup as hoggs in their first autumn and will lamb easily and make good mothers the following spring.

Providing their level of nutrition is maintained to ensure they have sufficient feed for the developing lamb to grow without hampering their own maturing process, such an early move into motherhood appears not to have deleterious consequences for these ewes. In fact, primitive-breed shearlings lambing for the first time often need careful shepherding to overcome bonding problems between ewe and newly born offspring. They may well initially appear totally shocked by the onset of lambing and adopt the 'drop and run' approach to parenthood. The best advice here is to make sure all shearlings are monitored closely at their first lambing so that otherwise strong and healthy lambs are not lost through sheer inexperience on the part of the shepherd and the ewe.

It is all too often forgotten that the ram is half the flock, so make sure he is in good order before he is asked to perform his annual task. If you have a stock tup, do not expect him to sit in the orchard gorging himself all summer and then turn into the athletic macho-male as soon as you open the gate and introduce him to the ewes.

Tups also need to be given a thorough overhaul before they start work. Their feet should be checked and they should be wormed, but it is also worthwhile checking their mobility and overall constitution. Stock rams can lead very sedentary lives, so make sure well in advance of tupping time that yours is well able to move around freely and serve his ewes. And it is essential at this time of year to turn the ram over and check his breeding apparatus. Both testicles should be of even size and feel firm. The sheath covering the penis should be free from any warts and the penis should also be extracted to check for abnormalities. Do not allow a ram to get too fat before tupping and aim for condition score 3.5 to 4.

The number of ewes that a ram will serve depends on the breed, but as a general guide a well-developed ram lamb in his first season as a sire should be able to successfully mate twenty-five to thirty-five ewes; mature rams could run with up to forty-five ewes.

Rams should be run with ewes so that they have the opportunity of mating the ewes over three consecutive heat cycles. There are two methods of identifying when ewes have been mated. The simplest is termed 'raddling' and involves the use of raddle powder, which can be bought from any agricultural merchant.

The powder is made into a paste using a thick oil and then smeared across the ram's breast bone so that ewes are marked on the hindquarter as mating takes place. This system does involve renewing the raddle paste at least every other day and although minimum interference to the flock is advised at this time, this is one job that has to be done. It is also important to have the utmost respect for rams at tupping time. Even the mildest-tempered ram can become an angry individual in the autumn and may well regard you, his once trusted friend, as an enemy to be forcibly driven out of the field. Take no chances and make sure unsuspecting children are fully aware of the dangers.

A less time-consuming method is to fit a harness which is strapped on to the ram. It carries a holder for a coloured crayon which similarly marks the ewes at mating. Crayons are available in different colours, to enable them to be changed every sixteen days.

This allows the flock owner to estimate the lambing date by the colour marks on the ewes. Some ewes may carry a second mark which means they have cycled again and have been mated. A large proportion of ewes carrying two marks may well suggest the ram is infertile and has not been 'stopping' the ewes at their first oestrus. If this is the case, a replacement ram must be found or a delayed lambing will result.

When you are sure all ewes has been mated, it is best to remove the ram and allow the flock to settle down. Ewes can be allowed to lose a little condition and perhaps drop down 0.5 of a condition score. In my own flock, with ewes lambing in late March, I have been known to carry on feeding 0.25 kg of a coarse ration until late December, introducing hay if necessary. Ewes may then have about five weeks without any trough feed; though hay would still be offered, depending on the weather and grazing availability.

If housing is available it may be preferable to bring sheep inside at some stage after Christmas even though lambing may be several weeks away. This very much depends on the individual circumstances of each flock.

In some cases it may be easier to manage a housed flock, or bringing sheep indoors may prevent poaching of heavy land and enable ewes and lambs to be turned out on to rested pasture in the spring. If a January or February lambing is planned, ewes will be better off brought inside to lamb and turned out soon afterwards if conditions permit. Always remember not to house ewes when they are wet because soaked fleeces do not dry off quickly indoors. Always choose a dry day to house your sheep.

It is important to remember that heavily pregnant ewes must not be 'turned' in the latter part of gestation so feet must be checked again before lambing and the ewes must also be wormed.

Ensuring in-lamb ewes receive the correct nutrition is essential. Not only will it determine how the unborn lambs develop but it will keep ewes in the right condition. This is vital, not only to prevent ewes becoming too fat, which can lead to difficulties at lambing, but also to supply the precise amount of feed to build up their body reserves and achieve a good milk yield. Keep a careful watch over the flock during mid-pregnancy: any ewes which appear to be losing too much condition should be singled out for special treatment.

In general terms, there is no need to start increasing feed intake until eight weeks prior to lambing. Allow 0.5 m of trough space per ewe to avoid bullying and overcrowding at feeding, and introduce concentrates at about 100 g a day six to eight weeks before lambing-time, gradually increasing the level each week until the ewe is receiving about 750 g by the time lambing is imminent.

Smaller, primitive breeds often start to leave feed as they become heavily pregnant and lambing approaches. This can be a dangerous time and a 'dip' in nutrition, particularly if the weather is bad and ewes are not grazing, can lead to twin-lamb disease. Ewes should always be fed twice a day in late pregnancy but splitting their ration into three feeds is recommended if ewes are reluctant to satisfy their needs from two trips to the trough.

Having successfully mated your ewes, got them through the winter and fed them correctly, the most important time of the year approaches as lambing-time looms.

Lambing-time

Hands-on experience is the key to successful sheep keeping.
While many management tasks for the small-scale flock owner
can be mastered and improved upon over the years, there is one
in which proficiency has to be achieved with more haste: acquir-
ing the skills associated with lambing-time. The flock's greatest
triumphs and most bitter disappointments can occur at this crucial time in the flock calendar. There is much that can be learned
by the first-time lamber by reading books and talking to more
accomplished shepherds, but this is one job where experience is
the key. For those who buy sheep but have never been present
when a ewe has lambed, there are several options to ensure that
your own lambing-time has a fair chance of success. Waste no
time in contacting your local agricultural college or nearest
branch of the ATB Landbase, both of which are likely to run
annual early-spring lambing courses. They are an excellent
means of tuition for the newcomer to sheep keeping and will
provide visual and practical training in readiness for the problems that all too often present themselves when lambing sheep.
But time may not be on the side of those who have made summer and autumn purchases of foundation stock of breeds like
Hampshire Down, Dorset Down, Suffolk, Charollais and Texel,
which traditionally lamb from December to February. In this
case, my advice would be to obtain as much guidance from
other, more established breeders before lambing-time begins;
make sure you have someone you can call if you do have a cri-
sis; and perhaps most importantly – remembering that other
breeders like yourself will also be in the throes of their own

lambing-time – ensure you have made contact with your vet.

Ask him to call round well before lambing starts so that he can familiarize himself with the breed and your set-up. It may well be that a particular partner in the practice is more experienced in sheep matters and if so, it is best to have him on 'red alert' well before the alarm bells start ringing. Some of the early lambing breeds are big sheep, dependent on concentrate-feeding and housing at a time when spring-lambing breeds are only just starting their term of pregnancy. Because of this rather specialized management, there can be more problems at lambing-time. While that is not meant to deter anyone from starting off with these breeds, it is essential to ensure that help is at hand.

Spring-lambing flocks, both those that may have to be housed for a short period and those lambing outdoors, will not be totally trouble-free but are likely to present fewer assisted lambings. But, as with any livestock enterprise, it is always advisable to assume the worst in order to be well prepared. In one sense, lambing-time is the beginning of new life, but in many ways it is also the culmination of your breeding plans and to lose lambs at this stage can be most frustrating – emotionally and economically. If you can locate a local farmer whose own flock is lambing before yours, it is always worth asking if you could lend a hand. You may only be given the tedious, unskilled jobs that are part of the hectic daily routine in the lambing shed but just being there, in a position to watch, listen and learn, will be of enormous value.

The Essential Kit

Well before the first lambs are expected, the new sheep keeper must ensure everything is to hand in readiness for the most hectic time in the flock calendar. The 'lambing kit' will become your lifeline; it must be a comprehensive collection of specialist equipment, veterinary items and lambing aids, some of which you will hopefully never need, but having them to hand for a 'dead of night' emergency could mean the difference between life and death for a ewe and her lamb. A container to hold the varied components of the lambing kit is an important consideration. While a cardboard box may seem like a good idea, it is totally unsuitable; tugged about with wet hands in the lambing shed, it will soon collapse and become useless, so opt for a strong wooden container or, better still from a hygienic point of view, use one of the plastic 'carry-all' boxes now widely available from hardware stores. Make sure there is a bucket to accompany the kit; washing hands in the nearest water trough is not recommended as the correct 'scrub-up' procedure before embarking upon the internal examination of a ewe. In fact, hygiene standards must be high at all times during any lambing procedures, so a thermos flask of hot water, antiseptic soap and towels should always be within reach. And so to the contents of the kit.

Lubricants

Over the years, shepherds have used a host of substances to achieve and maintain lubrication during an assisted delivery. The farmhouse kitchen used to supply copious quantities of margarine and lard, though soap flakes and washing-up liquid still have their devotees. While a well-soaped hand and arm remains relatively effective, antiseptic lubricant gels are now widely used and an ample supply should be to hand for lambing-time. Hands and arms should still be thoroughly washed in warm soap and water before any internal examination is made, even when a gel is used.

Lambing cord

An assisted lambing requires the shepherd to achieve maximum control. The slippery legs of an unborn lamb are often impossible to grasp. When assistance is needed and the legs or head need to be secured to ease the lamb from the ewe, a lambing cord must be used. The cord, which has a slip-knot loop at each end, should be cleaned with an antiseptic wash before and after use, to reduce infection spreading between ewes. If you have to call the vet out, always make sure he uses your own lambing cord and not one that might have been used in another flock. Some shepherds would never dream of using a specific lambing cord because of the risk of infection between ewes; their preference is for 'make-do' cords of baler twine, disposed of after use.

Towels

You can never have enough old hand-towels around at lambing-time. A vigorous rub with a rough towel can do wonders to invigorate a new-born lamb.

Antiseptic dressing

The navel of a new-born lamb must be treated immediately to prevent the entry of bacteria and the risk of joint-ill. Aerosol or spray dispensers of navel treatments are now available from agricultural merchants or your vet. Do not be afraid to use liberally.

Colour marker

Do not assume that because you only have a few sheep you will always know which lambs belong to which ewes. Mismothering can be avoided by making sure that lambs are marked as soon as they are born. Alternatively, you may wish to insert numbered ear tags, in which case you must acquire the tags and necessary applicator from your agricultural merchant.

Stomach-tube

An all-important part of your equipment. Easy to use once you have mastered the technique, the stomach-tube is invaluable in administering colostrum to weak lambs. Giving colostrum via the tube and not through a feeding bottle guarantees the lamb has received the colostrum.

Colostrum

The lamb's first milk from the ewe contains essential colostrum, which ensures the lamb has an adequate supply of antibodies to fight off infection. Use the stomach-tube for weak or orphan lambs. They will need to be given colostrum taken directly from the ewe, from colostrum already stored in the deep-freeze or a powdered replacement. If you are keeping colostrum in your lambing kit it will be one of the powdered replacements now widely available. It is not cheap, but do not cut corners on cost. The colostrum intake at this point in the lamb's life is crucial and only the very best is good enough. Check out powdered colostrums well before lambing-time begins and make sure you have plenty in stock. Ewes that have given birth to single lambs usually have ample supplies of colostrum, some of which can be milked out of one teat into a plastic cup and stored in the deep-freeze in 200 ml quantities. At your first lambing-time with single-bearing ewes it is well worth taking the time to 'milk-out' some colostrum; if it is not needed then, it will keep until the following year. Frozen colostrum should be thawed out to body temperature before use but must not be reheated in a pan. There is more on feeding colostrum in the chapter on lamb care.

Bottles and teats

Supplementary feeding may be needed and there may be orphan lambs, so have proprietary calibrated lamb feeding-bottles ready and always keep spare teats.

Needles and syringes

Have several 20 ml syringes at the ready and a supply of needles in case you have to inject ewes and lambs. Your vet will advise you on needle size but twenty-one gauge/five-eighths of an inch length needles are best for lambs and nineteen or twenty gauge/one-inch length needles recommended for ewes. I recommend disposable needles are used only once and that the correct disposal container for old needles is obtained from the vet.

Calcium borogluconate

This should be obtained from your vet and used under his guidance, but is something that you should have in stock. A most effective treatment when given as an injection for milk fever (hypocalcaemia) or magnesium deficiency (hypomagnesaemia).

Pessaries

Preferred by some as an antibiotic treatment to be inserted into the uterus after an assisted delivery, though in most cases an intramuscular penicillin injection is usually considered sufficient. Be guided by your vet and take his advice on where best to inject your ewes. The muscle of the upper hind leg is a popular injection site, but care should be taken here to avoid important nerves.

Rubber rings

If your breed has to be 'tailed', you will have to apply rubber rings to remove the lower part of the tail. If you are running commercial sheep, you will need to castrate all male lambs. Rubber rings and an applicator will be required.

A digital thermometer

This gives an important indication of a ewe's state of health and will pin-point problems if lambs are becoming hypothermic.

Spring balance and shopping bag

The best way to weigh lambs is to use a small spring balance with the lamb suspended in a shopping bag. I always like to weigh every lamb. The information provides a good guide to individual ewe performance and also to the way lambs develop.

In addition to these essential items, you should have at least two sheep halters, for moving or securing ewes; a torch; rolls of paper towels; a pair of round-ended scissors; chalk for marking lambing pens; penknife; pen and pad for making notes; and a transistor radio. The latter may seem an unusual requirement, but it is not simply to entertain the shepherd during lonely nights in the lambing shed. For ewes and lambs of early lambing breeds that have to spend several weeks inside, I find that a low-volume transmission of Radio 3 or Radio 4 left on twenty-four hours a day has a most beneficial, calming effect on the stock.

Make sure you have a bottle of long-acting antibiotic in the fridge. This should be obtained from the vet and used with discretion.

Countdown to lambing

If you are intending to lamb indoors, you will need to build lambing pens to hold the ewes and new-born lambs for about forty-eight hours. December to early January-lambing ewes can often stay outside until two to three weeks before lambing but much will depend on the weather, grass availability and the workload. Heavily pregnant ewes of these early lambing breeds are usually relieved to come inside and have food, water and shelter provided. As lambing approaches and ewes start to show the first signs of labour, they should be moved into an individual pen for the delivery.

These pens are best made of wooden or metal sheep hurdles; any home-made efforts should take note of the width between the horizontal rails of sheep hurdles; the gap should not be big enough to allow an inquisitive lamb to get its head stuck. The newcomer to sheep keeping should understand quite clearly that lambs have a 'death wish'. If they can strangle, hang, skewer, drown or decapitate themselves, they will. With whatever material you build your lambing pen or whatever you have in it, near it or hanging above it, check, check and treble check the likelihood of a lamb committing suicide. Lambs seem to like baler twine, that essential all-purpose material that no livestock enterprise could satisfactorily run without. Baler twine is often hung from the rafters of buildings as straw bales are unwrapped. I once had several strands hanging above a small stack of straw bales kept adjacent to a communal pen of ewes and lambs. While replenishing bedding I left the gate open and a lamb immediately scaled the stack and placed its head in the noose of a length of baler twine, slipped and – thanks to my intervention – failed to achieve death by misadventure. Lambs apparently like to fall into water-buckets and drown, so you should have these firmly hooked about a foot off the floor. Remember that lambs will get their heads wedged in the smallest of gaps and try all sorts of unbelievable ways of getting stuck, twisted and suffocated.

Lambing pens should be a minimum size of 6.5 ft x 3 ft (2 m x 1 m), with the lower 2 ft (0.75 m) to ground level made 'solid' with wooden sheeting. Commercial recommendations are to build one lambing pen per eight ewes in the flock. Much depends on how close together your ewes start to lamb, but for a twenty-ewe flock I would have four pens on hand with the ability to erect some straw-bale enclosures if necessary. Solid-sided timber pens are probably the best in terms of preventing accidents to lambs, though they are more expensive, reduce air circulation and can harbour more disease. Thoroughly disinfect all pens about two weeks before lambing-time and bed down deeply with straw. A free-draining stone base for the pens is recommended. If you are lambing in midwinter you may decide to use heat lamps. These can be hung in a corner of the pen which has one or two bars across to enable the lambs to 'creep under the heat'. Do not fry your lambs; heat lamps can be 3 ft (1 m) or higher off the floor and still provide adequate warmth. For housed ewes and lambs kept inside in midwinter, a heated creep area can also be provided in the main body of the building. This not only gives lambs extra heat but is a useful place to site the creep-feeders, ensuring that lambs are drawn to the feed in a warm and well-lit corner of the shed.

If your flock is lambing in late winter – late February to March – you may decide to keep ewes outdoors until about four to six weeks before lambing-time. April-lambing flocks should not need housing. If ewes are to remain outside for lambing, it is best to bring heavily pregnant sheep into a smaller paddock near the house so that a close eye can be kept on developments. Ewes will often lamb themselves in a quiet corner and if all appears to be going well it is often best to leave well alone until the delivery is complete. At that point you can gather the ewe and lambs for a thorough check, dip the navels, mark the lambs, inspect the ewe's udder for adequate milk and functional teats and let nature take its course. But it is always advisable to have some under-cover accommodation on hand in case of emergencies. If a weak lamb is born or you have to assist in the delivery, these jobs are better dealt with inside where a much closer watch can be kept on the situation. So even where hardy breeds are planned to lamb out-doors do not be caught out with nowhere to put a 'hospital case' in an emergency. A ewe thinking about lambing will show obvi-ous signs; she may begin pawing the ground, holding her head low, and making sudden movements as she feels the first mild contractions. The ewe will appear unsettled and may lie down and then suddenly rise to her feet again. Her under-belly will look heavy and the vulva will be swollen. If a hand can be slipped under the ewe, her udder should feel full and tight. Some of the most characteristic signs of the first stage of lambing include rais-ing the head, grinding the teeth and curling the top lip as the con-tractions intensify. At no stage should ewes be turned on their back for inspection, even in the later part of their pregnancy. All checks must be carried out with the ewe standing or lying down. Eventually, and this can take an hour or even longer, so do not panic, there will be a sudden rush of water from the ewe as the membrane surrounding the allantoic sac bursts. Often the mem-brane is not punctured and the water bag may appear intact, but by this stage it is a sign that the birth is imminent. Within around thirty minutes of the water bag appearing – much longer than this suggests you may have a problem – the nose and the two front feet of the lamb should appear if the presentation is normal. The transparent membrane that has covered the developing lamb usually tears at this point of the delivery; if it does not, it should be gently broken from over the lamb's nose as it makes its way into the world. Some ewes remain standing throughout the deliv-ery, others lie down. Do not force the ewe into any position; pro-vided all is progressing smoothly, leave her alone. Once the head and legs are visible, the rest of the body should follow quite quickly; do not worry if the ewe is standing and the lamb sud-denly shoots out on to the ground. As soon as the lamb is born, the ewe should be allowed to lick its offspring, but my first reac-tion is to make sure the lamb is alive and well and breathing. I usually rub the lamb vigorously with a towel, ensure that all the membrane is quickly removed from its nose and mouth, and check that the lamb has taken that all-important first gasp of air. Lambs, particularly large lambs, can often appear 'lifeless' after being born.

Your number one priority is to make sure the lamb is breathing regularly, so do not be afraid to give that rib cage a good rub to stimulate it. There are a number of useful techniques you need to be aware of if you have to swing into action to revive a lifeless lamb, and these must be applied quickly. I still believe that vigorous rubbing with a rough towel is one of the best stimulants, but inserting a small piece of straw into the nostril is a very useful 'irritant' that is well proven as an effective 'kick start'. While I would not advocate heavy handling of new-born lambs, they can withstand a certain amount of 'rough stuff' if it is a case of life or death. Holding a lamb upside-down by its hind legs and swinging it from side to side has saved many a lamb for me. Blowing into the lamb's mouth and moving a foreleg up and down can also encourage breathing to start. There are also proprietary stimulants now available on the market which can be useful. Of course the most drastic action to take is plunging the new-born lamb into a bucket of cold water. When I first saw this done to a lamb following a lengthy Caesarean delivery early one morning I was convinced it was nothing more than a bit of 'theatre' on the part of the vet. How wrong I was. The split-second headfirst plunge of the seemingly dead lamb did the trick and as I set to work to dry the sodden creature it gasped a breath – the shock tactics had worked.

In a straightforward delivery, a healthy lamb should try to raise its head very soon after birth. But I cannot stress how important it is to get the lamb dry at this stage, to minimize heat loss. I usually embark upon my rubbing–checking procedure with the lamb held under the ewe's nose so that she can join in any licking and sniffing, which all helps bonding, particularly with first-time lambers. Knowing what to do and how to do it all comes with experience, but there is nothing more satisfying than infusing the spirit of life into a lamb that, without your assistance, would have surely died.

Normal presentations of twin and triplet births should follow the same pattern. When the ewe has finished lambing and the lambs have been marked and navels dressed, the ewe's udder should be checked. Applying a downward action with forefinger and thumb to each teat should produce a stream of thick, yellow colostrum – a sure sign that she is able to feed her offspring. If lambs are weak, the colostrum can be milked from the ewe into a container and fed to the lamb via a stomach-tube; if this proves difficult – and some ewes are easier to milk than others – frozen or replacement colostrum should be used. I like to see lambs sucking as soon after birth as possible. A helping hand may be necessary, although too much interference can have an adverse effect, so it is best to give the lambs a chance to find their own way to the milk bar and only intervene if there are obvious difficulties. If you have very large pedigree ewes lambing indoors in midwinter and there is a risk that lambs could be lain on in the lambing pen – quite a common problem with inexperienced ewes – it is worth considering temporarily placing the lambs in a cornered-off creep area in the lambing pen under a heat lamp, making sure that the ewe can not only see her lambs but also lick them. Straw bales and timber-rails can be arranged to create the creep. Lambs can be taken out of the creep to feed and then put back every couple of hours. I have implemented this system successfully and have kept ewes and lambs 'split' for about forty-eight hours, after which time lambs are usually stronger and risks are reduced.

But this system can be time-consuming and it must be remembered that lambs will try everything possible to escape and get to the ewe; to avoid the catastrophe of a lamb getting stuck or wedged in the dividing creep-division, every care must be taken to ensure that there is nowhere for a tiny head or body to squeeze into to fulfil the 'death wish' inherent in many lambs. While it may seem heartless to split up a new family, even for a day, it is even more devastating to find that a ewe has inadvertently lain on her lambs simply through the lambs' inability to react quickly to her movements.

If you are lambing ewes outside, it is a good idea to designate a corner of the field as an outdoor 'lambing shed'. Arrange a few hurdles and straw bales to form makeshift pens; ewes can either be lambed in these or transferred after lambing if you feel you want to keep an eye on things for twenty-four hours. And if your land is exposed it is always worth strategically placing a few bales around the field so that ewes and lambs have some extra shelter. But be warned: unless you can properly secure two bales on top of one another – two fencing posts driven in along each side is the best way – do not stack them. Lambs love to jump on bales and bigger lambs can easily drag top bales off on to smaller lambs with fatal consequences.

Orphan lambs and weak lambs may need extra care and attention, so always have a box containing straw handy, or a blanket over which you can suspend a heat lamp. But remember that once you have taken a lamb away from the ewe for a period of time there is no chance she will accept it again. Hospitalized lambs are bound for the bottle or the milk machine, although adoption may be possible. Skinning a dead lamb and placing the skin on the lamb you want the bereaved ewe to accept is the most common practice, although the ewe will have to be restrained in the early stages of the new bonding procedure. One method is to have an orphan lamb on hand when a ewe known to be carrying a single lamb is about to give birth. If the orphan lamb can be briefly and discreetly placed at the rear end of the lambing ewe and allowed to be drenched in the birth fluid, she may well accept it as one of her own.

Afterbirth will appear some time following the birth; some ewes eat the placenta but any found in the pen or the paddock should be collected and buried.

If Things Start to Go Wrong

Lambing difficulties

If a ewe moves into the first stage of lambing but progresses no further after an hour of straining it may be wise to examine her very carefully. By gently inserting two well-lubricated fingers into the vagina (the ewe can be standing or lying), it should be possible to assess the way things are developing and what part of the lamb, if any, can be felt. This could be the first indication of a possible malpresentation but it is more likely to be a large lamb that just won't budge. At this point you can either call the vet, seek the help of a more experienced sheep keeper or decide to wait a little longer.

You have to learn to be patient when lambing sheep but you also have to learn when to move into action. The two-fingered assessment is not a difficult procedure but unless you have received some training or have previous experience, it is not recommended that a novice sheep keeper embarks upon an internal examination. Far better to seek professional help.

If you can establish that the presentation is normal (a head and two front legs) and that the problem appears to be the size of the lamb, and you are experienced enough to give assistance, things can be taken a stage further. By carefully drawing the forelegs forward in a downward movement (use the lambing cord if necessary by attaching a loop around the first joint of each leg) and coinciding your action with the ewe's strains, a satisfactory delivery should result. But some ewes take several hours to lamb. If you are unsure after your two-fingered check and over six hours have passed since the stage at which the vulva became swollen, the vet should be called. Although experienced flock owners learn to tackle many of the difficulties associated with awkward lambings and only call the vet as a last resort, I strongly advise that a newcomer call in the vet as soon as a problem is recognized or requests help from an experienced shepherd. The following descriptions of malpresentations and lambing problems are given as an identification guide rather than practical instructions. Do not attempt assistance if you are unsure of the procedure.

For those who have had some practical instruction in the correct method of undertaking an internal examination, here is an outline of some important points. I like to have a ewe laying on her right side; hopefully I will have an assistant who can keep her still while I 'scrub-up', washing hands and arms thoroughly. I now use an antiseptic gel and start off by applying a 'blob' inside the ewe's vagina followed by liberal amounts to my hand and arm. It is important to keep the hand cupped – and to make sure you have removed your watch or any rings – and then to carefully insert it into the vagina, through to the cervix and into the womb if necessary, until the position of the lamb is clarified. Only experience will enable you to make this assessment but you should be able to feel the position of the head and legs and, with the correct presentation picture in your mind, determine what sort of 'mishmash' of limbs needs sorting out before a satisfactory delivery can be performed. However, it is one thing to know what is wrong with the position of the lamb and quite another to perfect the technique of putting it right. I often think of the womb as a 'bran-tub' at a garden fete. You stick your arm in and after that you are working blindly but you at least have room for manipulation. So too with an internal examination of the ewe. In some, though not all, malpresentations, the intention is to bring the head forward and make sure that you have a nose resting on two front legs.

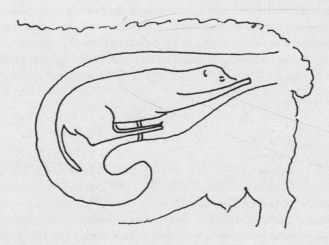

Figure 8a. Normal presentation

Let's take a look at some of the problems you may encounter.

Ringwomb

This could be a likely cause of the delay and is a result of the cervix failing to open up sufficiently to allow a normal delivery. The vet should be contacted and a Caesarean section may be necessary. There is another condition known as false ringwomb which can be corrected manually by inserting two well-lubricated fingers into the cervix. In most cases where a ringwomb condition is suspected, it is best to seek veterinary advice.

Head-first presentation

This can be a very awkward presentation to deal with, even by the experienced lamber. With the bigger breeds, particularly Down sheep, large-headed lambs seem more prone to this malpresentation. It can be especially traumatic if the lamb's swollen head is protruding from the ewe and there appears to be no sign of life. In this instance, the vet must be sent for immediately. He will 'up-end' the ewe and wedge her against a straw bale in order to replace the lamb in the uterus, correct the position and hopefully achieve a normal presentation, though lamb losses can be high. If the lamb's head is visible and the lamb is still alive, there is a better chance of its ultimate survival if the lamb is replaced in the uterus before the vet arrives to make a more complete correction of the delivery position. But this must not be attempted by a novice sheep keeper.

Head back

The feet are in the correct position but the head is twisted back. This can be easy to identify from an internal examination and is not difficult to correct, although it can be extremely frustrating when the head continues to slip back after being pulled forward. The lambing cord might be needed here.

One or two legs back

Some vets will attempt to deliver a lamb with a leg back but this is definitely not to be recommended for the novice. By applying internal pressure to the unborn lamb and pushing it back into the womb, it is usually possible to pull the legs forward into the

Figure 8b. Head-back presentation

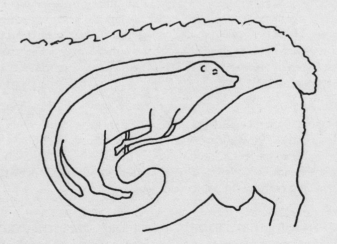

Figure 8c. Two legs back presentation

correct position, although if it is a twin birth care has to be taken to ensure the first leg and head you deal with belong to the same lamb. Experience will teach you how to 'crook' a finger behind a front leg to bring it forward and into the correct position. It is important to stress here than any manoeuvres involving 'sorting out' the presentation *must* be undertaken in the womb. There is not enough space in the cervix to start moving the legs and head about.

Breech birth

This is where the hindquarters of the lamb emerge first and in most novice sheep keepers it is where the alarm bells start ringing, when a tail appears instead of a nose and two front legs. I would always advise calling for the vet or other experienced help here, but for those who feel they can cope with this delivery the initial aim is to replace the lamb in the womb with great care. The hind legs can then be located and pulled forward so that they will be the first limbs to emerge, followed by the rest of the body delivered backwards.

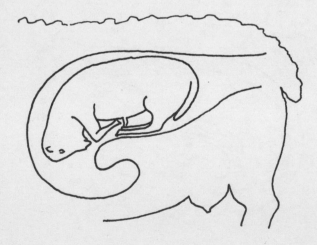

Figure 8d. Breech birth

These are just some of the variety of complications that can occur at lambing-time. If you do attempt any internal examination, you should make sure the ewe receives a routine injection of antibiotic to avoid infection. You cannot learn from a book or video how to lamb ewes correctly. Successfully overcoming a lambing problem is extremely satisfying, albeit stressful at the time, but it can only be achieved by experience. Most sheep keepers soon become sheep breeders and if that is your immediate aim the annual breeding cycle soon plunges you into lambing-time. So be prepared. Do not attempt to be James Herriot unless you feel totally confident. As soon as your sheep have arrived, book that lambing course. It will be a wise investment.

EIGHT

Lamb Care

*Dopey Lambs – The First Feed – Importance of Colostrum –
Stomach-tube Feeding – Colostrum Replacers – Colostrum Feeding
Rates – Ewe-milk Replacers – Docking – Castration – Care of Orphan
Lambs – Lamb Adopters*

Lambs are tougher than you think, though breeds do differ. I
never fail to be amazed by the hardiness of young lambs seen
skipping around fields frosted with snow in January. They have
obviously been born inside but after a few days of shepherding
indoors are well able to withstand the rigours of the New Year
weather providing they are on sheltered pastures. It is worth not-
ing here that lambs can withstand cold, dry weather far better
than a mild spell of persistent driving rain. Apart from what has
to go inside a lamb in the first few days, and we will come to that
shortly, much of the protection a lamb has from the cold is via its
fleece. Some breeds have better 'skins' than others in terms of
weather resistance; a few of the continental breeds have a reputation for producing lambs that could do with more wool to repel
the worst of the British winter weather. If you are breeding valuable pedigree sheep and lambing early in the New Year, you may
prefer to keep ewes and lambs indoors for several weeks. But
much depends on the breed and your location. Hardier hill and
upland breeds, primitive rare breeds and breeds which traditionally lamb in spring will happily cope with the whole process outdoors and their lambs will carry a good fleece and be inherently
active enough to deal with the weather. If your ewes and lambs
are outside and have shelter, do not panic and try to bring them
inside if they remain hunched up under a wall or hedge. You
should never house sheep when they are wet, and to bring sheep
in suddenly when the weather takes a turn for the worse is not
recommended. Providing the flock has shelter and the ewes are

feeding the lambs well, they will come to no harm unless extreme blizzard conditions or a flooded field threaten to take lives.

Whether your lambs are inside or out, there is a strict post-lambing routine that you should follow. Check new-born lambs all over – limbs, eyes, mouth – to ensure all is well. Spray the navel once the lamb is dry and make sure he can be identified (tag or mark as preferred). There is great variance in the way lambs of different breeds behave immediately after birth. Some breeds stagger to their feet within seconds and have a remarkable determination to get to the milk bar in record time. Others, mainly the heavier Down breeds, have a reputation for being 'dopey' and will simply lie motionless unless stimulated. Lambs that are active – the term 'sharp' is widely used to describe this type of lamb – usually present few problems in terms of achieving their first suck of the all-important colostrum. If the ewe is experienced and the delivery straightforward, the lamb or lambs should need no help in starting to feed. However, shearlings and hoggs (first-year sheep) lambing for the first time may be reluctant to let their lambs feed. With the ewe penned and bedded on clean straw, it is possible to hold lambs below the udder and gently place the lamb's mouth on to the teat, carefully drawing the teat down to provide the lamb's first taste of colostrum. It is possible to allow lambs to suck from a ewe that has been cast on her side and restrained in that position by a helper. Lambs will suck from this position and it goes some way to giving the lamb the genuine experience of feeding; the 'udder butting' stimulates the ewe to 'let down', in other words, release her milk supply. If a lamb is unable to undertake assisted sucking in the standing position, I usually prefer to use the stomach-tube and hope that within twenty-four hours its natural sucking tendencies will return. An unwillingness on the part of ewe to co-operate in allowing a lamb to suck can be most frustrating, but patience will pay off. If you have weak or hypothermic lambs which are unable to stand and suck and the ewe has lambed outside, I would recommend the family is penned, preferably inside, and the lambs dried, warmed and fed with colostrum via a stomach-tube.

Colostrum ensures that the disease immunity of the ewe is transferred to its offspring. It is a concentrated source of energy and also contains a laxative agent. To guarantee lambs receive this source of immunity and the required energy to maintain adequate body temperature, the correct amount of colostrum must be ingested within the first twenty-four hours. At least 25 per cent of this must be within three hours of being born. There are three main sources of colostrum: if a ewe is reluctant to feed her lambs or the lambs are weak, you could milk colostrum from her and feed it via the stomach-tube; it does not matter if a lamb receives colostrum from another ewe, so colostrum can be collected from other newly lambed sheep – say, those with single lambs – in readiness for an emergency. Alternatively, cow colostrum can be used, but in some cases this can cause anaemic lambs so it is best to discuss this source of colostrum with your vet. Colostrum replacers are also now widely used. They are not cheap but this is not a time to cut corners: buy the best you can and take advice from others about the range of brands.

Feeding via a stomach-tube

The main risk when using a stomach-tube is that it may be inserted into the lamb's windpipe, and for that reason great care must be taken, particularly when feeding very weak lambs. But the stomach-tube is a lifeline for many lambs. It is not a system of force-feeding but a guaranteed method of achieving the all-important colostrum intake when its direct extraction by the lamb from the ewe is not possible. They are readily available from agricultural merchants and sheep-equipment suppliers, and the stomach-tube procedure is easily mastered. If you are using frozen colostrum, it must be thawed (not in a microwave) and warmed to blood temperature. Draw the colostrum into the syringe and attach the plastic stomach-tube. Find somewhere comfortable to sit and lay the syringe and attached tube alongside you, making sure that it is within reach and laying on a clean surface to avoid any contamination of the tube itself. Take hold of the lamb and secure its position with one arm; its head should be held firmly in one hand, allowing the other hand to manipulate the tube. It can be tricky at first, but take things slowly. If the tube is warmed in a bowl of water it serves to soften the plastic and makes it easier to insert into the side of the lamb's mouth. Let the lamb start to take a couple of chews on the tube but at no stage insert it by force. Gradually slide the tube into the mouth until 50–75 mm (2–3 inches) is inserted. If any resistance is felt, it must be removed immediately. If the lamb shows any signs of distress the tube must be removed and the procedure restarted. If all has gone well and the tube has been inserted its full length into the stomach, I then like to withdraw by about two inches. At this point, colostrum can be administered by slowly depressing the syringe, taking about twenty-five seconds to deliver the contents. Stomach-tubes must be thoroughly washed after use and stored in hypochlorite solution.

Many commercial farmers, let alone small-flock owners, become very confused over the amount of colostrum required by new-born lambs. Lambs that are unable to take colostrum from the ewe or are too weak require three or four assisted feeds via the tube during the first twenty-four hours of life. The Ministry of Agriculture's guidelines should be followed, although it should be noted that colostrum levels should be increased by 20–30 per cent if lambs are outdoors and conditions are cold, wet and windy.

Lamb size/weight	per feed	per 24 hours
Single-born lamb at 5.5 kg	250 ml	1000 ml
Twin-born lamb at 4.04 kg	200 ml	800 ml
Triplet-born lamb	150 ml	600 ml

Small lambs born outside can soon become hypothermic. A useful technique to administer rapid energy to such lambs involves giving a glucose injection directly through the wall of the abdomen. This is a skilled technique and, though it can be mastered, it is advisable to seek veterinary help if you have never undertaken it before. Where lambs are weak and wet it is essential to follow a strict routine to achieve recovery. The lamb must first be thoroughly dried, then injected with a 20 per cent glucose solution warmed in a heater box or similar confined space, and fed colostrum via a stomach-tube *after* its temperature reads 38 degrees centigrade. Lambs treated in this way can often be returned to the ewe, though it is advisable to keep them penned for a day or two to keep a close eye on progress.

·Docking

Some breeds are docked and some live life with a full tail. Docking can be carried out using a rubber ring, or by the cauterizing method. Rubber rings are applied using an elastrator (obtainable from your agricultural suppliers); they are easy to use but care must be taken to ensure that the ring leaves enough length on the tail to cover the anus of male lambs and the vulva of female lambs. Legislation now covers this procedure, so it is better to be familiar with the welfare requirements in order not to end up with the severe docks reminiscent of the early imported breeds where the entire tail was removed. New cauterizing equipment now on the market makes this 'short, sharp shock' approach to docking worth considering, although you will need to have someone experienced to do the job for you. It always amazes me how lambs docked by this method appear to be totally unconcerned a few seconds after having part of their tails removed, clearly proving that the pain and distress level is minimal. I always like to spray the end of the newly cauterized dock with antiseptic although some say this is not necessary. The worst thing that can happen is that the gambolling lambs can lose the scab developing on the end of the cut dock. If this happens, severe bleeding can occur and infection can lead to joint-ill or stiffening of the limbs. If you do cauterize tails, always move around the sheep very quietly for a day or two to try to reduce the risk of lambs getting bumped or knocked.

Castration

If you are breeding pedigree sheep, chances are you will be expecting to produce a world-beater – and why not? Castrating male lambs is the last thing you will want to do. Male lambs that do not make the grade and end up heading for the butcher should not develop any 'raminess' as far as flavour is concerned if they are slaughtered before they would normally reach sexual maturity at five to six months old. So if you are breeding pedigree sheep it is normal practice to keep all your male lambs 'entire'. Those that fail to make the grade can be fattened for the freezer or sold *'in tacto'*. But if you are keeping commercial sheep you should castrate all your male lambs. It is a job that is best done when you are sure the lambs are strong enough – say, about two days old. It is a simple procedure involving constriction of the tubes leading to the testicles and is achieved using the elastrator. It is not a difficult job but help should be on hand from someone who is used to performing the task.

Orphan lambs

Caring for orphan lambs – either those who have lost their mother or whose mother has rejected them – starts off as a mission of mercy that all too often ends up being one of the most demanding and frustrating jobs associated with keeping sheep. Orphan lambs often end up far too 'humanized'. If male lambs are orphan-reared it is always best to castrate them unless they are likely to be truly outstanding. Adult rams that have been brought up on the teat can be a real danger when they mature. New-born lambs that are not going to be naturally reared must have adequate colostrum. After the first twenty-four hours, when you are satisfied that the lamb is thriving, its diet can be switched to a powdered milk replacer made up with water. The one thing you do not want to have to do is to spend hours – day and night – feeding orphan lambs, so the system I recommend achieves satisfactory rearing for the lamb and a minimum of stress to the shepherd. On day two, with the intention of getting four feeds into the lamb, I bottle-feed, making sure that the lamb has its last feed at midnight. I may continue this for two or possibly three days, depending on the size of the lamb and how it is responding. I tend to feed warm milk from the bottle until the lamb's appetite is really established but then the aim is to introduce the lamb to the ad lib system based on a cold mix of milk powder. This often seems a stark switch from the personal contact of a warm-milk feed from a bottle to cold milk sucked from an impersonal teated container, but if your lamb or lambs are thriving the transition can be remarkably swift. On the other hand, it can be fraught with problems; but that's what orphan lambs are all about, so be prepared.

Teated cold-milk lamb adopters are readily available from agricultural suppliers. Getting lambs to suck from them can take some time but my advice is to be firm. Try to fix up the adopter in a corner close to where you can hang up a heat lamp. The extra light and warmth often encourages lambs to stay close to the feeder for the first few days, and that is half the battle. You may find that lambs will have to be physically held to the teats for several feeds but gradually the penny will drop. Good-quality hay should always be on offer close to orphan lambs, who will nibble at hay after just a few days. After about a week I place a trough of lamb-creep pellets close to the milk bar; they will take very little at first, but gradually intake will increase. I am always keen to move on from the monotony of the pellet and introduce a lamb to a coarse ration. Lambs love to nibble at different textures and flavours of feed and you will notice a marked increase in intake once your feed becomes more interesting and the aroma of a molasses mix becomes irresistible. Water must always be provided for orphan lambs.

The cold-milk mix should be offered ad lib and adopter feeders cleaned out thoroughly every other day, making sure that the teats have not become clogged up with powder that has not been properly mixed. By six to seven weeks, the lambs can be weaned when you are confident they are taking plenty of dry feed. Weaning should be sharp. It seems harsh but it is the only way. By this stage, most lambs will have had some access to outside grazing, coming into a building for their supplementary feeds. It is up to you to decide if you wish to continue offering additional dry feed and will depend on how fast you need your lambs to develop. Unless you require sustained growth from January-born lambs that need to be ready to sell at pedigree sales in midsummer, most orphan lambs will thrive on grass and will relish the opportunity to join the main flock without any risk of bullying.

NINE

Sheep Health

*Vaccination – Needles – Pasteurella – Pregnancy Toxaemia –
Hypomagnesaemia – Hypocalcaemia – Mastitis – Swayback – Scrapie
– Sheep Scab – Coccidiosis – Louping-ill – Abortion – Liver Fluke –
Footcare – Roundworms – Tapeworms*

The shepherds of times past would have surely been agog at the
level of veterinary and health support that is now considered an
essential part of routine flock management. Much of it has
occurred during the transition of sheep keeping from its traditional 'dog and stick' image to a sector of British agriculture that
is now considered a flagship of our livestock industry. Increasing
output imposes pressure on any system of farming and with it the
risks increase. Although many of the stock tasks that must be
mastered to achieve sound sheep husbandry are identical to those
adopted by the shepherds of a hundred years ago, there are many
new animal health regimes and vaccination programmes that are
now considered the norm in everyday sheep keeping. As suggested earlier, a routine visit from your vet will set out a sheep
health plan for the year.

Vaccination

Sheep are at risk from several clostridial diseases, including lamb
dysentery and pulpy kidney. A simple programme of vaccination will now give protection which is maintained throughout
the life of the sheep by an annual booster dose. Lambs do gain
some protection from the ewe's colostrum but it is advisable to
inject lambs at some stage between six to twelve weeks old, and
to give the booster about four weeks later. In-lamb ewes should
be given a booster dose about six weeks before lambing,

although care must be taken not to stress ewes at this stage of their pregnancy.

Needles

Becoming proficient at injecting sheep is not difficult. Two types of injection can be given: subcutaneous (given under the skin) and intramuscular (given into the muscle). Over the years, I have seen farmers give injections at various points on the sheep's anatomy but the most widely used are on the upper part of the neck above the shoulder and in the rump area below the tail. Because there are serious risks from inadvertently injecting into a major nerve in the rump area, two other sites for injection are now being suggested by vets: the area at the front of the brisket just above the leg (an area often devoid of wool) and in the front of the thigh on the hind leg. Your vet will supply needles and syringes (which must be kept in secure storage) and you should discuss the appropriate needle size with him for the age of sheep you are dealing with. For subcutaneous injections, make sure that your needle is not too long or you will insert it under the skin only to find it pops out on the other side and jets the vaccine into the air! Adult sheep should not be injected with the same needle size used for cows. Hygiene must be a priority when injecting sheep. Needles used for routine vaccination can be used from sheep to sheep but after about ten jabs most needles are becoming blunt. If you are treating a sick sheep you can use the needle several times on the same animal (providing the needle is replaced in its cover between each use), but the needle should be destroyed when the treatment is complete. There are now strict rules governing the disposal of needles. Do not put them in the dustbin: ask your vet for advice.

Pasteurella

This is pneumonia in sheep and can kill them quickly. Stress, warm and 'muggy' weather, a sudden change of weather, or moving to new pasture or being housed can all spark off an outbreak of pasteurella. If you see a sheep 'puffing' through

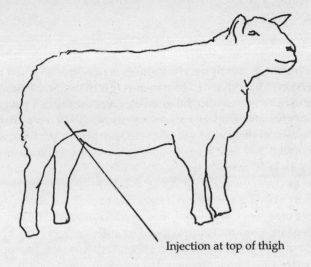

Injection at top of thigh

Injection site just in
front or just behind
front leg

Figure 9. Injection sites

laboured breathing, it is possible that you have spotted the first signs of pasteurella. Even though some of the multi-clostridial vaccines contain cover against pasteurella, it is no guarantee that pneumonia will not strike. Protection will only last for about six months and in young lambs for around six weeks. Older lambs may require further pasteurella cover at around three months old, but your vet will advise you. In many cases, the speed with which pasteurella can affect a ewe leads to death simply because it has been impossible to spot the problem quickly enough. If you suspect pasteurella you must ring the vet immediately. A course of antibiotics can save the day if you act swiftly.

Pregnancy Toxaemia

Most commonly known as 'twin-lamb disease' and most likely to occur during the month before lambing and in ewes carrying twin or triplet lambs. During this late stage of pregnancy where multiple births are expected, there are heavy demands being made on the ewe, which is why it is essential to take great care over feeding and management, particularly in ewes which are wintered outside and if there is a high proportion of older ewes in the flock. It is essential that ewes are carefully monitored at this stage of the year. For out-wintered flocks, a sudden snowfall or hard frost can deprive ewes of feed at a critical stage of lamb development. The drain on the ewe's body reserves caused by nutritional stress can quickly lead to the onset of twin-lamb disease. Symptoms are a desire to stand away from the main flock, and possibly twitching, with head held low or to one side. The ewe will behave in a 'stupid' fashion and her eyesight may even be affected. The disease is sometimes referred to as 'snow blindness'. After a couple of days, if not treated, the ewe will be unable to stand and will soon die. Ewes carrying too much condition can also suffer from the disease because excessive internal fat inhibits the ability of the ewe to ingest sufficient food. Treatment for ewes close to lambing is limited and death may often result, but the vet should be called. He may well advise the sticky job of trying to get the ewe to take treacle – this can be done with a wooden spoon and a lot of patience. Treatment may also include a multivitamin injection.

Hypomagnesaemia

Low blood levels of magnesium can lead to hypomagnesaemia which is often seen in newly lambed ewes, particularly if they are turned out – with all the best of intentions – on to a lush spring pasture. Nitrogen fertilizers applied to boost grass growth can have an adverse effect by 'locking' magnesium levels in the soil and so depriving the sheep of its uptake through grazed grass. Twitching and stiffness of gait are the symptoms and death will result if the ewe is not treated. Ewes can also suffer from magnesium deficiency during the winter. Treatment often leads to a swift recovery. Ewes should be treated with 100 cc of magnesium solution given subcutaneously. For small ewes, the 100 cc dose can be given in several different injection sites to improve the rate of uptake.

Hypocalcaemia

Often referred to as 'lambing sickness', this disease occurs in the later stages of pregnancy and most often in older ewes. The cause is calcium deficiency as developing lambs make demands on the ewe for bones and teeth. Affected ewes may 'stagger' about, lay down, stop eating and show signs of breathing difficulties. Response to treatment can be rapid if ewes are given a subcutaneous injection of 100 cc of a 20 per cent solution of calcium borogluconate.

Mastitis

Lactating ewes are always at risk from mastitis. There does not appear to be any rhyme or reason why a particular ewe should be affected. It is assumed that a ewe will regulate her milk production for the lambs she has to feed, but for some reason single lambs often prefer to take milk from one side only, a situation that soon leads to a mastitic condition on the other side of the udder. Thick teats can also be the cause of mastitis as lambs find it difficult to suck and either leave milk in the udder or concentrate on the smaller teat of the two. Mastitis can occur at any stage of lactation. Good milking ewes whose lambs are taking more grass or feed and less milk should start to 'dry off' by themselves but this does not always happen. The first signs are a swollen and hard udder which becomes inflamed. Attempts to draw milk usually produce a thick, clotted liquid, sometimes stained with blood. Veterinary advice should be sought and an antibiotic treatment will be prescribed. It is likely that an affected quarter will never be functional again and although the ewe could suckle lambs with one teat, you should seriously consider culling her.

Swayback

Sheep and excess copper are a lethal combination, which is why it is essential never to feed concentrates formulated for cows (containing copper) to a flock of ewes. Although sheep do require some copper if they are found to be deficient, the dosage is critical. Veterinary advice should be sought. Swayback is caused by a lack of copper in the diet and usually affects lambs from three weeks old. A lack of co-ordination of movement and stumbling action are tell-tale signs. Lambs may suffer mildly for weeks or death may occur quickly. Seek veterinary attention.

Scrapie

A virus disease which has become widely debated following the BSE issue affecting British cattle herds. It has occurred in sheep flocks for generations but official 'scrapie-monitoring schemes' now under way in breeds most susceptible have substantially reduced its incidence. The scrapie virus attacks the brain and spinal cord and produces a nervous condition. The 'itching' and rubbing against posts and fences displayed by infected sheep is characteristic of the virus. Sheep in this condition start to lose their fleece and body condition deteriorates. Symptoms can last for weeks or months but always end in death. There is no cure, but research is now finding ways of selecting breeding stock which is genetically resistant to the virus.

Sheep Scab

There are calls for this disease to be made notifiable once again. The scab mites cause irritation in the fleece and on the skin of affected sheep, leading to serious loss of body condition and even death. A strict dipping programme will prevent the occurrence of scab in the flock. Small-flock owners may well wish to dip their sheep with a neighbouring farmer when he undertakes the job in his own flock. Alternatively, you could contact a mobile dipper to visit you and dip on site. Always ensure that your sheep have been properly dipped and that they are totally submerged and remain in the dip bath for the required time. Care must be taken when handling dipped sheep. There are now Health and Safety guidelines concerning the use of dip and its disposal. Your local MAFF office will give you all the information you need.

Coccidiosis

Most commonly seen in housed lambs with scouring as the first sign. Loss of condition will follow. This parasitic problem can also occur where lambs are stocked heavily on pasture. Notify your vet if you suspect coccidiosis, but if you are feeding creep pellets to housed lambs, make sure they contain a coccidiostat.

Louping-ill

Much research is still under way into this tick-borne virus which is transmitted to sheep after being bitten by ticks. Sheep on hill and upland grazings are most at risk but pour-on treatments – a method of pouring a concentrated dip solution along the back of the sheep – have brought about a big improvement to the tick problem on many farms. Louping-ill is recognized by the 'trembling' behaviour of infected sheep which gradually causes paralysis of the limbs. Vaccination is now proving successful.

Abortion

This refers to the premature birth of lambs and can be devastating to the small flock if hit by an abortion 'storm'. There are two main types of abortion that the small-flock owner needs to be aware of: toxoplasma and enzootic abortion.

Toxoplasma is a parasitic type of abortion which is spread through oocysts passed in cats' faeces. Ewes usually slip their lambs in the later stages of pregnancy. There is no treatment, but immunity following such an abortion is generally good. Any foetuses or afterbirth must be taken to the vet immediately for diagnosis.

Enzootic abortion is caused by a virus and causes lambs to be lost from mid-pregnancy onwards. It can be brought into a flock by buying in infected sheep or lambs and will erupt at lambing-time. Vaccination is now a successful method of control but ewes that abort will automatically be immune to infection in future lambings and need not be sold.

Liver Fluke

Most common in wet summers and on land that tends to be boggy. It is caused by a parasite. The liver fluke life cycle is complex and involves the mud snail. Sheep grazing grass containing the encysted stage of the fluke cycle become infected. The immature fluke travels through the sheep's gut to the liver where it feeds. Its eggs are passed out with the sheep's faeces and the whole process takes about twelve weeks. Sheep show symptoms of listlessness, lose condition and display pale eyelids. Worm drenches can now be given which contain a flukicide, but breaking the life cycle of the mud snail can also be achieved by running a few ducks on pasture which is at risk – ducks love to eat mud snails!

Foot-rot

Sheep seem to enjoy being lame and some breeds enjoy it more than others. Good standards of footcare are an essential part of flock management and must be mastered as a priority. Foot-rot is a general term for a wide variety of foot problems in sheep. The characteristic foul smell associated with foot-rot makes for easy diagnosis once the bacterium has taken hold and sheep have become lame. Sheep should be upturned and the feet examined closely. The skin between the claws of the foot may seem inflamed or the problem may have spread to the tissue of the sole of the foot or even beneath the horn of the claw. Practical guidance should be sought from someone experienced before the novice attempts the following procedures. Using a pair of sharp and clean foot-shears, the careful job of paring away the horn to expose the infected area should be undertaken. Further treatment with antibiotic spray may help but exposing the infection is the prime aim. Swelling or heat in the foot should be noted and a more detailed veterinary diagnosis may be necessary. Scald is another foot problem often referred to alongside classic foot-rot. This is interdigital dermatitis, causing very painful red and moist inflammation between the claws. As for foot-rot, it can be treated with antibiotic spray but prevention is the key to reducing foot problems and it can be achieved by regular checks and frequent use of the foot-bath. These shallow troughs can now be bought from agricultural merchants and placed in a narrow 'race' so that sheep have to stand in the bath for the required time. Running sheep through a foot-bath has little benefit. It is essential that sheep are allowed to stand for several minutes in the solution to receive its full benefit. Zinc sulphate added to water is the safest to use. For those who do not own a foot-bath, a degree of success can be achieved – if you have only one or two sheep to treat at a time – using a bucket containing zinc sulphate solution. You may also need a helper and a co-operative sheep. You will hopefully end up with a sheep with better feet but your own back pain will encourage you to invest in a purpose-built foot-bath as soon as finances allow!

Do not assume that all foot problems are treatable with the foot-shears. If you feel unsure about diagnosis, call the vet. A lame sheep is bad enough, but a dead sheep is even worse.

Roundworms

An effective programme of treatment to control worm burdens in sheep is vital. Nematodes are a major threat to sheep health so it is important that every flock sustains its attack on worms. Worm eggs passed in the faeces of infected sheep develop into larvae, attach themselves to grass and are eaten by more sheep to maintain the cycle.

Worm infestation of sheep is a complicated matter and a system of clean grazing – only running sheep on the same pasture in alternate years – is effective when sufficient land is available. But if the small-flock owner adopts a regular worming programme and worms ewes before tupping time, about three weeks before lambing, and worms all lambs at grass every three weeks from spring until autumn, a good level of worm control should be achieved. Sheep suffering from worms will lose condition, scour and often cough repeatedly. Resistance to some anthelmintics (the treatment for worms) has been proved. To reduce this problem, manufacturers now offer 'white' and 'brown' wormers to give sheep keepers the opportunity to use a different type every year.

Tapeworms

This problem is most commonly found between June to September. An intermediate host – a tiny mite – is involved in the infection process. Sheep pass infected droppings on to the pasture; these contain egg-filled worm segments which disintegrate, releasing the eggs for the mites to pick up. Grazing lambs take in the mites containing the tapeworm cysts and continue the cycle. Many sheep seem to cope with tapeworms with no ill-effects, although some heavy infestations will cause pot-bellied lambs and a loss in condition. Anthelmintic treatment will cope with the problem.

TEN

The Shepherd's Calendar

*Month-by-month Guide to the Sheep Year – Vaccination
Programme – General Flock-management Tasks – Lambing
Preparation Timetable – Shearing Date – Dipping Times – Worming*

September

A good time of year to start the calendar. The end of the summer
heralds the sale of the season's lamb crop and the arrival of flock
replacements, possibly a new ram and, for the first-time sheep
keeper, the purchase of foundation females. This is the month
when the main sheep sales get into top gear. They will last until
November, but for anyone buying foundation stock there is no
better time than early autumn to buy sheep. The weather is still
good enough to allow new stock to settle down before the winter
takes hold and before rams are turned out. And there should be
plenty of opportunity for new sheep keepers to familiarize themselves with their stock, moving quietly among them or just sitting
close by. Ignore any strange looks from passers-by; if your sheep
know you and feel confident in your presence, life will be a lot
more straightforward in the depths of winter and at lambing-time
when you need to be on good terms in times of trauma. It does no
harm to have a bucket on your arm. A few handfuls of feed can do
a lot to build confidence in sheep and the sooner your presence is
associated with feeding-time, the better. You may not have
enough sheep to warrant a fully trained sheepdog or you may be
keeping one of the primitive breeds which are notoriously difficult to 'herd' in a forward direction without splitting in all direc-
tions. A useful tip is to adopt a familiar call when you approach
your sheep. If they link this with feed then you will soon have an
element of control that will be forever useful. Avoid choosing a
black or green bucket for carrying feed. Opt for bright blue or yel-

low and always stick to the same colour. Some say sheep are colour-blind but the sight of our bright blue bucket – empty though it might have been on occasions – would usually bring ewes running from the other side of the field.

When your new sheep arrive – whether from a private source or from a sale – it is advisable to worm them as a precaution. Ask the breeder if they have been vaccinated. If not, you should give a clostridial jab to provide protection from clostridial diseases. This is a good time to get to know your vet too. Invite him to come and check over your sheep and ask his advice on a year-round health programme. His experience of sheep keeping in your area will be invaluable. You should have checked teeth and feet – and udders in ewes that have already sucked lambs – before you bought them, but this is a good time to have another look at feet and to pare any overgrown horn. Dipping is no longer compulsory and you are unlikely to have dipping facilities at home. If you definitely want them dipped against parasites and have bought sheep privately, you should make your request clear before you take delivery. There are now several pour-on treatments on the market that claim to provide the same cover as immersion dipping by pouring concentrated liquid along the back of the sheep. This would be the best time to administer such a treatment. Any dip products need to be used at least six weeks before the tups are turned out. If you are running a conventional spring-lambing flock and you intend to put the tups with the ewes in mid-October (for lambing to start in mid-March), you may wish to start some supplementary feeding in September, but much will depend on the condition of ewes, as discussed in the chapter on preparing for lambing. Buy in sheep feed but not too much – it is better to buy small quantities, to keep it as fresh as possible. This is a good time to buy in hay; you will get the best deal if you can haul it straight off the field. Buy as much as you need to last for the entire winter; hay only gets dearer as the winter progresses. Consider investing in a tarpaulin to cover the stack which will last for many years. There is nothing worse than having paid for good hay only to have it ruined when your makeshift 'cover' blows away in an overnight gale.

October

Keep a close eye on ewes and make sure they are on a rising plane of nutrition during the run-up to tupping. Trace-element blocks should be available – I always find ewes take more from their mineral blocks at this time of year. Rams will need to be having a daily ration of about 0.25 kg (0.5 lb) depending on the breed but care should be taken not to get them too fat and lazy. You may decide to raddle your ewes, which certainly takes the guess work out of lambing-time. The raddle crayon will tell you when each ewe has been mated; change the colour of the crayon every seventeen days – the interval between heat cycles.

November

Continue to feed ewes if you are supplementing at tupping time and if grass is getting short. Offer hay in racks – sheep will waste much of the hay if it becomes wet and trampled on the floor – should the weather deteriorate.

December

You may have decided to house your sheep for part of the winter and this may be the month you wish to do so, but make sure you do not bring wet sheep inside. Choose a dry day but try to leave sheep out as long as possible unless pasture is suffering from poaching.

January

Get your lambing kit together and remember that clostridial injections and worming will be necessary six weeks before lambing begins. I do not advise injecting and worming on the same day, as this can lead to excess stress. Do not inject sheep on a wet day. Ask around to see if you can lend a hand on a local farm where lambing is already under way and check up on lambing courses at your local agricultural college or ATB Landbase office.

February

The first crocuses and snowdrops should gladden the heart of every shepherd as springtime is just around the corner. But this is a critical time of the sheep year. It is a good time to speak to your vet and if necessary request a routine flock health-check. Put him on red-alert for lambing. Make sure you have plenty of colostrum in stock as well as ewe-milk replacer. These checks should all be included in the seasonal overhaul of the lambing kit. Ewes that go lame must not be 'turned-up' for footcare so late in pregnancy. Turn feet up as a blacksmith would shoe a horse; it is a two-handed job and be careful not to stress the ewe. Lambing pens need cleaning and checking. Build or buy new hurdles and repair old ones, and make sure you have plenty of straw in stock to provide deep beds for lambing ewes. Ewes will need to be fed for six weeks prior to lambing. Provide enough trough space to avoid competition between ewes.

March

Probably one of the busiest months of the year. Be prepared for long nights in the lambing shed. Once lambing has started there needs to be someone on hand twenty-four hours a day to supervise the flock. Cancel all squash matches and trips to the hairdresser: this is the real thing. If you feel like treating yourself and you are lambing ewes inside, you could indulge in a closed-circuit television. They are not totally foolproof but at least you can check ewes more regularly without leaving the house. Once ewes have lambed and mother and family are settled and feeding, you can worm the ewes and check their feet before turning them out into a sheltered field.

April

The grass should be growing, the birds should be singing and you should be catching up on some sleep. If all has gone well, you can start feeling pleased with yourself. If not, this is a good time to make a few notes about where things went wrong so that similar problems can be avoided next year. Check every ewe and her lambs each day. I start worming lambs from six weeks old. Lambs need their first clostridial injection at around ten weeks old and the second four weeks later.

May

A wonderful month for the sheep keeper. The summer shows are starting and your flock should really be in full bloom. Keep an eye on dates for the lambs' first clostridial injection and if you consider there is a risk of orf you may want to check with the vet about orf treatment, which involves a 'scratch' of serum on the lambs' skin.

June

Shearing will already have begun in many flocks. Cold May nights for newly shorn ewes can reduce milk output, but by early June most sheep are ready to be rid of their fleece.

July

The end of this month should see some lambs weaned and the ewes taken away and wormed. In small flocks, where land may be limited, a less rigid system can operate. My primitive ewes which lamb in April remain with their lambs until the day before the lambs are sold (starting in early September), but it is advisable to insert a 'dry-cow tube' of penicillin into the teats of ewes immediately after the lambs are taken off. These can be obtained from the vet.

August

Ewes taken away from their lambs should be given a thorough check. Any that have succumbed to mastitis, leaving them with damaged udders, should be marked and any others with obvious problems that may result in them being culled should be identified. Ewes that have milked well but are in poor condition should be given good grazing and extra feed if necessary in readiness for the cycle to start all over again.

ELEVEN

Showing Your Sheep

*Selecting Sheep for Show – Feeding for Show Condition – Trimming
and Preparation – Show and Halter Training – Showing Essentials*

Showing sheep can be enormous fun, but like anything competitive it can have its disappointments. If you do decide to show
some of your sheep you must take victory and defeat with the
professionalism of a true livestock showman. You may have
bought some sheep with 'show potential' or you may have begin-
ner's luck and breed something really good, but you should
always remember that it takes as much time and effort to get a
good sheep ready to show as it does a bad one. Only show your
best and do not attempt a half-hearted turnout. Your reputation
will be won or lost by the type of sheep you show, so it is better to
wait until you really have something worthy to exhibit. If that
takes a year or two, the time will not be wasted. Attend as many
shows as you can and you will be surprised how much you will
learn from watching and listening.

Apart from the basic requirements of good conformation and
good health, every breed has its own standard. These are points
that are particular to that breed and may relate to the type of
wool, the colour, or the size, right down to the length of tail or the
ear carriage. If you are considering showing some of your sheep
you should make sure they have as few faults as possible.
Outstanding sheep of all breeds have their day but the perfect
sheep has never been bred. All sheep have faults but top winners
have fewer than those that stand down the line. By talking to
other breeders and by standing at the ringside and comparing
your selection with that of the judge, you will gradually learn the
art of selecting sheep for the showring.

Every breed has its own set of regulations, laid down by the
breed society concerned, affecting the way sheep are prepared for

the ring. Down breeds like the Suffolk and the Hampshire Down, as well as the Jacob, require many hours of skilful trimming to create the traditional fleece shape and texture required for the ring. Other breeds like the Texel are shown naturally and are not 'dressed' with shears; and the hill breeds and primitive sheep are similarly shown either fully clipped or 'in the wool' depending on the time of year and the age of the sheep. Whatever your breed you will have to familiarize yourself with its showring 'style'. Most breeders are only too pleased to help newcomers to showing and are happy to pass on a few tips that will enhance your chances of winning.

Not only do all breeds have different requirements when it comes to their outward appearance for the showring. Breeds like the Suffolk, Charollais and Texel require careful feeding for many weeks in the run-up to the show season. The aim is for the sheep to reach the peak of condition by show day. Overfeed them and you will end up with nothing more than a fat and probably very sick sheep; underfeed them and they will lack condition and be passed over by the judge. It is a fine line but it is one that many top sheep exhibitors have spent a lifetime perfecting. While big breeds will readily take several pounds of feed a day as part of their pre-show conditioning, others would soon become ill if fed such generous rations. Some books have tried to be specific about rationing sheep for the showring but there is such wide variance in sheep breeds that it is far better to seek independent advice from fellow exhibitors of your own particular breed.

A very experienced friend of mine who has spent a lifetime showing sheep at the highest level at major shows throughout the country believes that sheep easily become bored in the run-up to the show season. Penning them in a small paddock and lavishing them with up to four feeds a day may seem like paradise to those on the other side of the fence but it is very easy for the 'show team' to become unexpectedly lacklustre. This can be very demoralizing for the new exhibitor. One cause is feed: pelleted feed offered in large quantities can be a monotonous diet so try varying the ration. If you watch sheep eating something they like you will notice that they often roll food around in their mouths, almost playing with it. The varying constituents of a molassed coarse mix provide an interesting diet that is always well received by sheep. Barley is the key to putting weight on sheep but care has to be taken not to overfeed. Whole oats of good quality are always relished by sheep; they will not put a lot of weight on a sheep but they will keep the appetite sharp and are a good conditioner. Sugar-beet shreds are another favourite, though I always prefer to feed them after they have been soaked overnight.

There are other ways to alleviate boredom. Providing you are well fenced and can keep control of your sheep, it is a good idea to take them for a walk at night. A nice steady trot for ten minutes will keep sheep in tip-top form. The exercise not only encourages sheep to empty themselves several times – always good for their constitution – but also firms up their muscles and keeps their movement sound. During the stroll, sheep should be allowed to browse grass and herbage along the way. Many people forget that sheep are selective grazers and while a lush field of grass may seem like every ewe's dream come true, it too can become monotonous. If you do walk your sheep you will be surprised just how many times they stop and take a nibble at a whole variety of plants and grasses. Always make sure sheep being prepared for show have ample supplies of fresh water and a mineral block and that they have been wormed. Feet, too, will need attention. Horn seems to grow more rapidly when feeding levels are increased, so keep your foot-trimmers close by. Trim feet at least a week before the show and not the day before, just in case your best sheep takes umbrage and ends up feeling sore.

Show Training

Some people find training sheep for the showring one of the most stressful and arduous of tasks for both sheep and handler. There is no doubt that it can lead to frayed tempers and the more uptight the handler becomes with an unco-operative sheep, the less likely he is to achieve success. I actually enjoy training sheep for the showring; I consider it a great challenge and the more dif-

ficult the sheep, the more I enjoy it. Breaking the confidence barrier is the key. Most sheep, even those that may push at the trough
and nuzzle you in the field, take on a whole new personality once
they have a halter on their head. On one occasion, because I had
been very busy in the few weeks before a big show, I had failed to
spend any time show-training a six-month-old ewe lamb I had
great hopes for. Two days before the show, I placed a halter on
her for the first time. The reaction was explosive, to say the least,
but after about an hour, even though she was far from what many
people would consider halter-broken, I decided I had done
enough. At the show I placed the halter on her again for only the
second time in her life; we walked into the ring and she not only
won a class of over thirty entries but went on to be reserve champion. Many of the other entries were totally untrained, so I had to
smile to myself as a fellow exhibitor said to me: 'You had better
lead everyone out, yours is the only one that is halter-trained.'
How it is done is very difficult to explain, but a few words of
guidance will hopefully help the novice.

First, catch your sheep and place the halter correctly on the
head with the nose-knot on the left-hand side of the sheep's face.
Adjust the knot so that it is not a 'running-knot' and will not automatically tighten as the sheep resists. Armed with a bucket of feed
and a bucking sheep, move away from the rest of the flock to a
quiet area where there are no distractions. Make sure the sheep
knows what is in the bucket; offer feed by hand and talk quietly
and reassuringly. At this stage, if you try to take a step forward,
leading the sheep, the animal will simply pull back and probably
jump in the air. After this first show of resistance I usually begin
what I consider to be the crux of successful halter-breaking.
Taking a firm hold to ensure the sheep cannot suddenly rear up
and knock me in the face – particularly unpleasant if it has horns
– I begin to blow gently down the animal's nose. Over the next
half an hour I will repeatedly blow down the sheep's nose, I will
sit down with the sheep close to me, I will stroke the animal
around the head and face and generally accustom it to my touch,
smell and voice. Even after some time there is still likely to be
resistance shown by the sheep every time I give it the opportunity

to walk on the halter. It will leap forward or sideways and prove most awkward. But suddenly, and this moment comes with experience, you can sense a very slight change in behaviour, a minor lessening in resistance. At this point I often give the sheep the full length of the halter rope. As it begins the 'stop–start' procedure I may well invoke the 'go away, I am not your friend' approach. The outcome of briefly alienating myself from the sheep, combined with the bond already created by nose-blowing, continues to build the relationship between sheep and handler. The turning point comes when you can actually get the sheep to walk towards you. It is too daunting for the animal to attempt this while you are standing over it. Sit down about two yards away, facing the sheep. Priming it with more nose-blowing, quiet encouragement and even a little food, coax the sheep gently towards you. If you can get just one step from it, you are well on the road to having a fully trained show sheep. The rest will follow on with patience and kind handling. Remember that most sheep have no confidence in humans other than a realization that they can provide food and shelter. On most occasions a sheep is handled only to inject it, worm it, trim its feet or pull out a malpresented lamb: all very traumatic. You cannot tell a sheep that all you want it to do is to wear a halter and walk by your side. All you can do is achieve a rapport that will engender confidence and trust between sheep and handler that will hopefully prove to be a successful showing partnership.

At the Show

You will need to plan your showing well in advance. Find out the names and addresses of the show secretaries organizing the events you want to attend and apply for a schedule. Although the county shows and the 'Royals' carry the most coveted championships, start off at your local show and cut your teeth on home ground. Alter the routine of your show sheep as little as possible in the few days before the show. Check with your local Ministry of Agriculture office about livestock-transport regulations. These are being tightened all the time so it is best to be fully aware of what documentation you need to carry in the car as a record of your travelling times. Make sure you have feed, hay and buckets for the stock while they are at the show as well as your 'show box', which should contain several essential items. Many will be specific to your own breed but the all-important white coat, halters, brushes, towels and first-aid requirements for you and your sheep should be packed. Learn how to stand and show your sheep to ensure its qualities are clear to the judge. If it is a big class you may want to let your sheep relax while the judge examines the other entries, but never take your eyes off the judge. He may well come back to look at your sheep at any time so you should always be aware of his whereabouts. When it comes towards the end of the initial assessment he will probably take a broad sweep of the entire class and it is then that you should have your sheep looking 'spot-on' in readiness for the first phase of the final placings. By all means converse with your neighbour in the ring, but never lose sight of why you are there and keep your eye on the judge. He may just catch a glimpse of your sheep standing badly and that could throw away your chances.

Read the schedule carefully. It will contain all the information you need to know about arrival times and judging times. Remember that no two judges share the same viewpoint in every detail and a win at one show does not guarantee victory at the next. Enjoy the camaraderie of showing and never leave the ring without congratulating the winner. It is never a bad thing to remember that no one forced you to come; by entering, you sought the judge's opinion of your sheep, whatever that might be.

TWELVE

The End Product

The public's perception of wool never fails to surprise me. It is widely considered that wool is the primary source of income from sheep. How wrong this view is. It may well be the high price of woollen garments that engenders it, but as I assume most readers of this book will be aware, wool sold to the Wool Marketing Board will not generate sufficient income to make keeping sheep for their fleeces a viable option. While there are those who do make more than others out of the wool produced by their sheep – either through its quality, by selling yarn or making clothes – meat production is the primary source of income from commercial sheep.

If you are running a flock of sheep for purely commercial reasons you should choose a breed to suit your circumstances, with the aim of producing good-quality prime lambs. You will probably opt for a Mule or Half-bred ewe and use a terminal sire breed such as the Suffolk, Texel or Charollais. Mule and Half-bred ewes are well proven as good mothers and milkers which will breed a good number of twin lambs. The good conformation of the wide range of terminal sire breeds available will impart the correct 'shape' and leanness to the progeny to suit the needs of both consumer and butcher. The crop of lambs, both male and female (though it is usual to castrate the males), should be suitable for the modern prime-lamb market. When you sell, at what weight and where, will depend largely on when you lamb, the breeds you are dealing with and your location. Winter-born lambs, while more costly to produce, usually command a high price in the weeks up to Easter. Spring-born grass-fed lambs of the Suffolk cross Mule type should be ready for market at around 40 kg live weight in late summer. Another option is to sell lambs as 'stores', enabling others to buy them and run them on for several more weeks or even months until they have attained marketable condition.

Those sold until Christmas are still classed as 'lambs', but sheep sold between January and late spring are termed 'hoggets'. Prices for hoggets in spring can be very high but much depends on having the ground to carry them on over the winter and the ability to feed them in the last eight weeks before sale to achieve the correct level of fleshing, known as 'finish'.

If you are producing a commercial crop of lambs, you may decide to sell them at your local market which will have one day a week – usually a Monday – as the main day for selling all prime stock. You will need to check the time of the sale and any other arrangements because many auctioneers like to start early in the day so that buyers can complete their orders and stock can be transported quickly to their destination. Alternatively, you may choose to sell 'dead weight'. This means marketing your lambs through a slaughter company which will have to be contacted well in advance to see if the lambs you have to offer meet the tight specifications of weight and finish that they demand for their discerning supermarket customers.

Local butchers may well be interested in your lambs, so you should make contact with them to see what they require. This should be done well ahead of any lambs being ready for sale; in late summer it is not difficult for lambs to become over-fat, a condition that will reduce their value and make them harder to sell. Depending on how many lambs you have to sell, when you are lambing and what breed you keep, private sales of 'freezer lamb' to friends and family can often turn into a thriving business. You will have to arrange to have the lambs slaughtered – the local NFU office or neighbouring sheep producer can usually supply information on this – and then to have them butchered. Most local butchers will provide this service for a fee, though if your lambs are good enough you may well find that the butcher himself starts to take an interest in your lambs for his own shop. From the butcher, you will collect the entire jointed carcass and the offal but it is useful to discuss with him how you want the carcass butchered. The latest butchery techniques can produce some very attractive joints and steaks, so make sure he knows exactly what you need.

If you keep rare breeds or are producing prime lambs by crossing two breeds that are not widely available commercially – say,
Ryeland cross Shetland (which incidentally produce a top-quality
carcass lamb) – the family and friends option can be extended to
restaurants and hotels. As with selling to freezer customers,
lambs marketed to hotels and restaurants will have to be
butchered, but you will often find that many chefs welcome with
open arms the chance to chalk something up on the specials board
like 'locally reared Manx Loghtan lamb' – and they will often pay
a good premium over the market price.

The Rare Breeds Survival Trust has also launched a marketing
scheme to assist small-scale flock owners to sell their stock. It
operates by diverting supplies of rare-breed meat to specialist
retail outlets. While excellent in theory, in practice the scheme can
be inconvenient if you only have a few spare lambs to sell because
you may have to take them to one of the RBST's approved finisher
units from where they will eventually be sold; unfortunately,
there are still only a limited number of these units and a long journey may not be worthwhile if you only have a couple of lambs.
But there are plenty of opportunities for entrepreneurs to get
together and market their lambs as a joint venture, either to private customers, to butchers or restaurants. Joining forces and
increasing the number of lambs you have to sell serves to guarantee a level of supply – something that restaurants prefer if they
find you have a product that is popular with their clientele.

It is important to make sure that any lambs you sell for human
consumption are fit and healthy and that they are well past any
withdrawal period if they have been treated with any medication
in the weeks prior to slaughter, and that includes worm drenches.
You will have to make a special request to have the lamb skins
returned to you as many butchers and slaughter houses retain
these and the value is allowed for in the charges made.

Even if you are running a pedigree flock of whatever breed,
there are likely to be sheep, particularly males, that do not
develop into quality breeding animals. This poses the question of
castration. Normally you would apply the castration rings soon
after birth but if you have a pedigree flock it is impossible to tell

at such a young age which male lambs are going to turn out to be world-beaters. With pedigree lambs born in the winter to breeds such as Texel, Suffolk and Charollais you should be able to make a reasonable judgement on quality and breeding potential by twelve to sixteen weeks old. Anything that is clearly not up to standard should be sold as a prime lamb as soon as possible. The fact that these lambs are entire should not have any adverse effect on flavour and eating quality and should not lower their sale value. However, 'raminess' does produce a taint to the meat of older male sheep that are left entire.

Pedigree breeding is probably the main aim of most small flocks. The newcomer to sheep keeping often finds it difficult to learn whether it is males or females of particular breeds that command the highest prices. Apart from the very best rams, most of the primitive breeds achieve the highest prices for female sheep, whereas in breeds like the Suffolk and Texel – apart from top-quality breeding females – it is the rams that command the highest prices. Your surplus pedigree stock can be sold at special sales held throughout the country each autumn, many organized by the breed societies; and there is always a ready market for well-bred commercial 'crossing tups' of the popular breeds which are needed by farmers, principally to produce butcher's lambs. You may decide to retain some of your females or to enter some for one of your breed society's sales. Sheep breeding is first and foremost part of our agricultural industry, and because farmers depend on sales being organized to dispose of their stock and to buy in new sheep, an extensive 'marketing framework' is in place. This provides a year-round system which is equally open to large- and small-flock owners.

Rare-breed supporters have the Rare Breeds Survival Trust's main autumn sale held in September each year as well as several regional fixtures. By selling at auction you can always place a reserve on your stock to ensure you receive a fair price, but returns from sheep can be variable.

All sheep, with the exception of the Wiltshire Horn which does not grow a fleece, must be sheared once a year. There is a trend among some commercial flockmasters to shear in-lamb ewes when they are housed, but for the small-flock owner the early summer clip will be the one most widely practised. While it is possible to master the art of clipping sheep, there are now plenty of contract 'clipping gangs' offering their services. New flock owners must contact the Wool Marketing Board well in advance of clipping time to obtain information concerning the marketing options for fleeces. This will enable your registration to be processed and sacks provided in which to pack your fleeces while they await collection. The small and often variable income from wool can be enhanced. There is a market for black and coloured wool, and Shetland sheep breeders maintain a thriving interest in the high-quality wool produced by their stock. British wool varies widely in quality. Coarse wool, almost hair-like, is produced by breeds such as the Rough Fell and is excellent for carpet-making; Yorkshire wool from breeds like the Wensleydale has a lustrous sheen and is highly valued by cloth designers; and Shetland wool, with its fineness and variety of colours – eleven main whole colours of fleece – is renowned for top-quality knitted garments and famous lace-knitted shawls.

Hand spinning has enjoyed a great resurgence in recent years and you may well decide to choose a breed that will provide high-quality or coloured wool, or, as with the Shetland, both these qualities. Breeds like the Shetland, the Jacob and the Hebridean, to mention just three, are outstanding examples of sheep that can provide their owners with good-quality prime lambs, either crossed or pure; coloured wool to sell or spin; and possibly an income from selling top-quality pedigree stock.

Many small-flock owners embark upon keeping sheep by buying a couple of ewes to act as lawnmowers in a paddock or an orchard. Many casual starts such as this have been the foundation of a life-long fascination with sheep breeding. Not only is there a huge number of breeds to consider, but the new flock also has the potential to be at least self-financing through the challenge of the many marketing options that can be pursued for meat and wool.

Glossary of Terms

aged/senior an old ewe probably six years old or more

barren ewe a ewe that has failed to breed

carding comb used to lift the wool on the sheep in preparation for show trimming

chilver used in the south-west to describe female sheep

condition the body weight or amount of flesh being carried by a sheep

couple ewe and lamb

creep an area sectioned off to allow lambs to graze but preventing access to ewes or an area containing special feed for young lambs

crimp the 'wave' that appears in some wool fibres such as the fleece of the Wensleydale

cross-bred sheep that have parents of two different breeds

cuckoo lambs lambs born after 1 May

dagging/crutching trimming away soiled fleece from the tail area. Usually undertaken prior to tupping and lambing

double ewe and twin lambs

draft ewe a ewe still fit to breed from, but being sold from the flock. Used mainly for hill flocks when sheep are sold at a certain age to finish their productive life on lowland farms

dry ewe one that is no longer lactating

finish used to describe the level of body condition in relation to a lamb's readiness for slaughter

finished lamb a lamb that has reached the correct weight and body condition to be sold for slaughter

flushing improving the nutrition of ewes before tupping, usually by moving the flock to fresh grassland. Undertaken to increase ovulation

fly-strike attack by flies which lay eggs in the skin and fleece. Maggot infestation can result

full-mouth a mature sheep showing eight broad teeth at four years old

gigot another term for the hindquarter area of a sheep. In terminal sire breeds, this is very pronounced and muscular and suggests the ability to pass on this trait. It is a highly desirable quality that will hopefully be passed on to prime lambs sired by terminal sires used in commercial flocks

Half-bred specific term for sheep sired by the Border Leicester (English Half-bred, Welsh Half-bred)

hoggets/hog first-year sheep between six months and one year. Comes into use after Christmas when describing prime stock

in-breeding mating sheep that are closely related

in-bye land on hill farms that is lower in altitude, usually surrounding the farmstead, giving the best grazing

kempy wool term referring to the harshness of wool fibres found in some breeds

killing out percentage the amount of saleable meat produced by a carcass

lambing percentage the number of lambs born to a flock. A more relevant figure is the number of lambs reared

life ewes with lambs at foot often sold in spring at auction at a price 'per life'

line breeding a skilful method of breeding pedigree sheep by bringing bloodlines together of similar ancestry without mating stock that is too closely related

Mule specific term for cross-bred sheep that are sired by the Blue-faced Leicester (North of England Mule, Scottish Mule, Welsh Mule)

notch a mark cut in the outer edge of the ear as an official identification procedure in some breeds

oestrus the period when ewes are in mating condition

scour diarrhoea

shearling, yearling, two-tooth, gimmer, theave sheep that have been sheared once and have two broad teeth

stock sheep sheep that are established within a flock and are proven breeders of good progeny

store lamb potential slaughter lambs that have not yet been put on to their final feeding regime that will add the necessary weight and condition to sell them as prime stock

tag a plastic or metal tag clipped through the ear with special pliers as an official means of identification. All sheep must now carry some form of identification

tattooing official marks tattooed in the ear for registration purposes of some pedigree breeds

three-shear sheep showing six broad teeth at three years old

tup/tip male sheep

two shear sheep showing four broad teeth at two years old

wether, teg, wedder castrated male sheep

Some Useful Information

Modern Breeding Jargon

Signet – the animal-breeding division of the Meat and Livestock Commission – offers a sheep-breeder service to enable pedigree-flock owners to use the latest genetic index data for flock improvement. Many of the terminal sire breeds are now involved in these schemes and an increasing number of commercial farmers are buying rams 'with figures'. This refers to data on estimated breeding values which indicate an animal's genetic strengths and weaknesses. To find out more, you should contact Signet at Signet Farm Business Consultancy, PO Box 603, Winterhill, Milton Keynes MK6 1BL.

Maedi Visna Accreditation

Many newcomers to sheep keeping are initially confused by the term 'acc' and 'non-acc' when referring to stock. The terms denote whether or not stock is accredited; in other words, it has been bred in a flock which is blood-tested and has been found free of maedi visna – a virus of Icelandic origin which attacks the lungs. A large number of pedigree flocks are now classed as 'MV-acc' following the introduction of accreditation schemes by breed societies. The MV scheme is now being run by SAC Veterinary Services which will provide full details: SAC Veterinary Services, West Mains Road, Edinburgh, EH9 3JG. Telephone (0131) 535 4000.

Livestock Transport

New legislation affecting the transport of livestock has been introduced which not only affects the time spent travelling but also the mode of travel. Close attention is paid to the suitability and cleanliness of the trailer being used and to maintaining details of journey times which must be carried in the vehicle. If you are going to be moving sheep on a public highway it is in your own interests to become fully conversant with the law.

Identification

All stock now has to be identifiable. Pedigree stock has to be registered with the appropriate breed society but non-pedigree animals must now be tagged so that their origins can be traced. Although it is now necessary to keep up-to-date records of all sheep bought and sold, this level of record-keeping is also an important aid to good flock management. It should be extended to provide an individual lifetime 'ID' card for every sheep in the flock, to enable information to be held concerning breeding performance and veterinary attention.

Sheep Quota

If you have a registered agricultural holding, or you apply for such status through your local MAFF office, you may be entitled to sheep quota. This enables you to claim an annual cash payment on your sheep, known as the Sheep Annual Premium Scheme. Full details of how to obtain quota and explanatory notes on sheep premium payments are available from your local MAFF office.

Meeting the Market's Needs

If you intend to produce prime lambs, it is essential that you learn how to assess their condition and flesh cover and to estimate their weight. Handling live lambs for this purpose is an acquired skill gained by regular practice. The 'dock' – the tail root – and the 'loin' – the area on either side of the spine – are the two main areas. Individual bones in the tail of the lamb should be discernible; the fatter the lamb gets the harder it is to detect bone structure in the dock. As with condition scoring, described in an earlier chapter, the less prominent the transverse processes of the spine, the fatter the lamb. You are advised to study the Meat and Livestock Commission's information booklets on selecting lambs for the market which give full details of the conformation grades (E,U,R,O and P) and fat levels (1,2,3L,3H,4L,4H and 5). While some lambs will fall into the top categories for both conformation and fatness, they are the exception rather than the rule. Striking a balance to achieve lambs at 2–3L at U conformation grade is considered quite acceptable, but it is essential to be fully conversant with the needs of your market.

Useful Addresses

The British Wool Marketing Board, Oak Mills, Station Road, Clayton, Bradford, West Yorks BD14 6JD (01274) 882011

International Sheepdog Society, Chesham House, 47 Bromham Road, Bedford MK40 2AA (01234) 352672

Ministry of Agriculture Fisheries and Food, 3 Whitehall Place, London SW1A 2HH

The National Farmers Union, 164 Shaftesbury Avenue, London WC2H 8IIL (0171) 5807172

National Sheep Association, The Sheep Centre, Malvern, Worcestershire WR13 6PH (01684) 892661 (will provide details of membership and a list of all breed societies)

Rare Breeds Survival Trust, National Agricultural Centre, Stoneleigh, Warwickshire CV8 2LG (01203) 696551

The Royal Agricultural Society of England, National Agricultural Centre, Stoneleigh, Warwickshire CV8 2LZ (01203) 696969

Index

abortion, 86
advertising of sheep sales, 3
afterbirth, 65
aggression, 7–8
agricultural colleges, 54
agricultural contractors, 26, 27
agricultural shows *see* showing
    sheep
Agriculture and Development
    Advisory Service (ADAS), 46
agro-chemical herbicides, 27
antibiotics, 60
artificial feeding, 58, 74–5, 77–8
artificial insemination, 44
ATB Landbase, 54
auctions, 2–3, 4

Bakewell, Robert, 9–10
barley, 40, 41, 98
Beltex sheep, 21, 23
Berrichon du Cher sheep, 21, 23
Beulah Speckled-face sheep, 21
birth *see* lambing
Black Welsh Mountain sheep, 21,
    40
Bleu du Maine sheep, 21, 22–3
Blue-faced Leicester sheep, 10, 14,
    21
bonding problems, 50–1, 65
Border Leicester sheep, 10, 14, 21
boredom: avoidance of, 97–8
Boreray sheep, 21, 43

Brecknock Hill Cheviot sheep, 21
breech birth, 70
breed societies, 3
breeds of sheep: Continental, 21,
    22–4; hybrid, 19–20; Jacob, 16,
    18, 21, 97, 106; Longwool,
    14–15, 21; mountain (hill)
    breeds, 11–12, 21; rare, 15–16,
    21; selection of, 1, 2, 9–24;
    Shortwool, 13–14, 21;
    Shortwool Down, 12–13, 21
British Friesland sheep, 23
British Wool Marketing Board,
    102, 106, 113
broken mouth, 5, 7
butchers, 103
buying sheep: points to look for in,
    5–8; sheep sales, 2–5, 90, 105

cabbages, 41
calcium borogluconate, 58–9, 83
calcium deficiency, 83
Cambridge sheep, 19–20
Camtex sheep, 20
Castlemilk Moorit sheep, 16, 21
castration of lambs, 59, 76–7,
    104–5
Charmoise sheep, 21, 23
Charollais sheep, 10, 21, 22; breed-
    ing cycle, 44; feeding and
    nutrition, 38, 41; housing, 31;
    lambing, 54; sales of, 2–3, 105;

glossary of terms, 107–9
grain feeds, 40, 41, 98
grass-seed companies, 26
grazing, 25–8, 38–9; clean grazing
    system, 26, 88; fertilizer use,
    27–8; paddocks, 25; re-seed-
    ing, 26; weed control, 27

Half-bred sheep, 4, 10, 13, 14, 19,
    44
halters, 99–100
Hampshire Down sheep, 2–3, 12,
    21; breeding cycle, 44, 50;
    lambing, 54; showing, 97;
    stocking rate, 27
hay, 27, 28, 39, 78, 91
hay-racks, 37, 39
health care, 79–89; ewes, 8, 47,
    48–9, 82–4, 95; footcare, 35, 47,
    87–8, 91, 98; lambs, 72–8
heat lamps, 61
Hebridean sheep, 15, 17, 21, 43,
    106
hedges, 29
herbicides, 27
Herdwick sheep, 10, 11, 21; breed-
    ing cycle, 43–4, 50
Hill breeds, 11–12, 21
Hill Radnor sheep, 21
housing, 31–7, 92; ewes, 31, 32, 37,
    52–3, 60–2; flooring, 35, 37;
    reasons for, 31–2, 34–5; tem-
    porary shelters, 31, 34; types
    of, 35–7; ventilation, 35, 36–7
hybrid breeds, 19–20
hypocalcaemia, 83
hypomagnesaemia, 83
hypothermia, 75–6

identification marking, 57, 73, 111
Île de France sheep, 21, 23
in-field handling systems, 30
injections, 58, 80, 81
in-lamb ewes: sales of, 2–3
International Sheepdog Society,
    113

Jacob breed, 16, 18, 21, 97, 106

Kerry Hill sheep, 13, 21

lamb(s): abortion of, 86; artificial
    feeding of, 58, 74–5, 77–8;
    birth of see lambing; bonding
    problems, 50–1, 65; care of,
    72–8; castration of, 59, 76–7,
    104–5; 'death wish' of, 60–1,
    64; feeding and nutrition, 28,
    41, 73–5, 77–8; marking of, 57,
    73, 111; meat production,
    102–5; tailing of, 59, 76; vacci-
    nation of, 49, 79–80; weighing
    of, 59
lambing, 54–71, 92–3; birth
    process, 61–5; lambing cords,
    56–7; lambing courses, 54;
    lambing kit, 55–60; prepara-
    tion for, 54–5, 60–5, 92–3;
    problems in, 65–71
Leicester Longwool sheep, 9, 15,
    21
Lincoln Longwool sheep, 14–15,
    21
liver fluke, 86–7
livestock transport regulations,
    101, 110–11
Llanwenog sheep, 21
Lleyn sheep, 10, 13–14